MYTH AND SYMBOL

MYTH AND SYMBOL

Critical Approaches and Applications

By Northrop Frye, L. C. Knights
and others

A Selection of Papers Delivered at the
Joint Meeting of the Midwest Modern
Language Association and the Central
Renaissance Conference, 1962

Edited by Bernice Slote

UNIVERSITY OF NEBRASKA PRESS · Lincoln

Thanks are due the *Virginia Quarterly Review* for permission to include "*The Golden Bough*: Myth and Archetype"; to Archibald MacLeish and Houghton Mifflin Company for permission to quote from Mr. MacLeish's *J. B.: A Play in Verse,* copyright © 1958 by Archibald MacLeish; and to Martin Foss and Princeton University Press for permission to quote from Mr. Foss's *Symbol and Metaphor in Human Experience.*

Library of Congress catalog card number 63-9960

International Standard Book Number 0–8032–5065–7

First Bison Book printing: June 1963

Most recent printing shown by first digit below:

4   5   6   7   8   9   10

Manufactured in the United States of America

FOREWORD

The essays in this book may be called approaches to a critical method. Taken together they comprise an experiment in criticism: by repeated views from somewhat different vantage points, they present definitions and illustrate forms of a comparatively new way of considering literature—a concentration on myth and symbol. There is, of course, no clear-cut school of myth and symbol, and so we must admit in the beginning that in such criticism the meanings of even the key words are various. *Myth* refers sometimes to classical story, sometimes to created forms of belief; or it may function as creative or symbolic metaphor. Myth embodies archetype; it also borders on allegory. In the same way, the meaning of *symbol* often overlaps on other terms. For example, a symbol may be said to relate two or more elements, but so do metaphor and myth. As a start on unity, it may be helpful to summarize the premises and implications of the fifteen essays included here.

Regardless of terminology, there are certain consistent elements in these essays. The emphasis, first of all, is on the doubleness of literature—that what is given in language and form is only the embodiment of something more that is not, that cannot, be wholly stated. If we simplify definitions, we may say that a symbol contains both a literal reference and a much greater range of unwritten meaning, implication, and emotion. Imagery, form, and action may all be symbolic. Symbol often merges with archetype, or the expression of various universal, instinctual motifs or patterns of human behavior and belief that come charged with primary emotional force. Myth, both traditional and created, is the narrative form of those particularly archetypal symbols which together make a coherent revelation of what man knows and what he believes. In its doubleness, myth is vision objectified; it exists in terms of what is deepest in the springs of human feeling and perception. In all of the essays which follow, the critical search is for that which, though unspecified, exists in and through the word, and which makes the living design of the work of art.

In this criticism there is, second, an emphasis on the creative act. Because the critic is discovering design and meaning through the primary forces of human action, he is likely to find himself a closer participant in the shaping of a writer's vision. Such participation, says Northrop Frye in the opening essay, assumes that both art and criticism are in a "continuous process of creation." As Blake saw it, there is no distance between the creative power of shaping the form and the critical power of seeing the world it belongs to: "The vision inspires the act, and the act realizes the vision." L. C. Knights speaks also of "*the* creative movement of all literary form." In his view, there is capacity for change and renewal in all art, and an obligation of criticism is to recognize "the perpetually renewed meaning of any poem." Mr. Knights sees the work of art as one which "sets in motion those powers of apprehension through which we simultaneously become aware of, and make, our world." Thus consideration in literature of archetypal or symbolic framework, or the operation of myth, may in a special way remove the barriers between critic and creator.

In the following essays, fifteen critics have explored various interpretations through a study of myth and symbol. The opening section, "Critical Approaches," presents two major statements by Northrop Frye and L. C. Knights, both of whom have had personal impact on the direction of contemporary criticism. To Mr. Frye, through his work on Blake in *Fearful Symmetry* and his compendium of critical theory in *Anatomy of Criticism*, is generally attributed the beginning of interest in archetypal studies in literature. Mr. Knights, in his work on Shakespeare (*Some Shakespearean Themes, An Approach to "Hamlet,"* and others) and in recent studies of metaphor, has emphasized literature as theme and movement. In his essay the term *metaphor* is used in a broad sense, as "the making of a living image of experience that goes beyond the immediate representation." These are personal essays. With them are two other reviews of critical approaches: Eva M. Kushner's presentation of Gaston Bachelard's work in the psychology of imagination and his study of the elements as symbols, and Herbert S. Gershman's account of Surrealism as a movement that was itself creating new myths.

The "Applications" in the second and third parts of the book have a generally unified critical approach. The first essays take some samplings of writers and their methods: John T. Nothnagle, Thomas G. Winner, and Colin C. Campbell view and evaluate the handling of myth by Agrippa D'Aubigné, Chekhov, and Archibald MacLeish, respectively. The last two essays in this group consider particular devices. Robert L. Hiller discusses Brecht's symbolic use of *gestus*, or non-verbal expression, in the mimesis of a play on the stage. Sister M. Joselyn examines the implications of Katherine Anne Porter's use of animal symbolism in the delineation of human life. In this method, says Sister Joselyn, Miss Porter implicitly creates the non-human and partially human levels through which the protagonists struggle to grasp meanings and fulfill themselves.

In the second group of applications, the critic turns to the work itself. The first four essays look for a total design in a work through archetypal patterns. Eric LaGuardia, with an approach similar to that of L. C. Knights, sees *All's Well that Ends Well* as a dramatic metaphor of the regeneration of man. William M. Jones and Charles T. Dougherty study archetypes and interpretations in Milton and Ruskin, respectively. Alexander C. Kern in his essay on Faulkner's "The Bear" evaluates both the mythic and symbolic elements in the work and other criticism with the same approach. The final essays diverge in two ways: Warman Welliver's interpretation of Dante's *De Vulgari Eloquentia* illustrates the symbolic doubleness of the more fixed form of allegory, yet it shows in its own way the creative movement possible in this kind of symbolic structure. The final essay by John B. Vickery joins myth and literature with a slightly different perspective. If myth can be organic in literature, so our most notable direct expression of myth, Frazer's *The Golden Bough*, can be organic *as* literature.

If the essays in this symposium cannot make final definitions, we hope that even in their incompleteness they suggest the possibilities and illustrate the vitality of criticism concerned with myth and symbol.

Thirteen of the essays in this volume were selected from sixty-one papers delivered at the joint meeting of the Midwest Modern Language Association and the Central Renaissance Conference in April, 1962. The central theme of the meeting was criticism in relation to myth and symbol. The essays by Northrop Frye and L. C. Knights were originally presented as major lectures during the conference.

In the editing of *Myth and Symbol*, we have simplified many references by placing page numbers in the text and by combining citations whenever feasible. Unless otherwise stated in the notes, translations from languages other than English are those of the author of the essay.

BERNICE SLOTE

University of Nebraska

CONTENTS

Foreword, *by Bernice Slote*   v

CRITICAL APPROACHES

The Road of Excess, *by Northrop Frye*   3
King Lear as Metaphor, *by L. C. Knights*   21
The Critical Method of Gaston Bachelard,
    by Eva M. Kushner   39
Surrealism: Myth and Reality, *by Herbert S. Gershman*   51

APPLICATIONS (I)

The Writer and His Method

Myth in the Poetic Creation of Agrippa D'Aubigné,
    by John T. Nothnagle   61
Myth as a Device in the Works of Chekhov,
    by Thomas G. Winner   71
The Transformation of Biblical Myth: MacLeish's Use
    of the Adam and Job Stories,
    by Colin C. Campbell   79
The Symbolism of *Gestus* in Brecht's Drama,
    by Robert L. Hiller   89
Animal Imagery in Katherine Anne Porter's Fiction,
    by Sister M. Joselyn, O.S.B.   101

APPLICATIONS (II)

The Work Examined: Archetypes and Interpretations

Chastity, Regeneration, and World Order in
    All's Well that Ends Well,
    by Eric LaGuardia   119

Immortality in Two of Milton's Elegies,
  by William M. Jones   133
Of Ruskin's Gardens, *by Charles T. Dougherty*   141
Myth and Symbol in Criticism of Faulkner's "The Bear,"
  by Alexander C. Kern   152
The *De Vulgari Eloquentia* and Dante's Quasi After-Life,
  by Warman Welliver   162
The Golden Bough: Impact and Archetype,
  by John B. Vickery   174

CRITICAL APPROACHES

THE ROAD OF EXCESS

Northrop Frye
University of Toronto

It will be easiest for me to begin with a personal reference. My first sustained effort in scholarship was an attempt to work out a unified commentary on the prophetic books of Blake. These poems are mythical in shape: I had to learn something about myth to write about them, and so I discovered, after the book was published, that I was a member of a school of "myth criticism" of which I had not previously heard. My second effort, completed ten years later, was an attempt to work out a unified commentary on the theory of literary criticism, in which again myth had a prominent place. To me, the progress from one interest to the other was inevitable, and it was obvious to anyone who read both books that my critical ideas had been derived from Blake. How completely the second book was contained in embryo in the first, however, was something I did not realize myself until I recently read through *Fearful Symmetry,* for the first time in fifteen years, in order to write a preface to a new paperback edition. It seems perhaps worth while to examine what has been so far a mere assumption, the actual connecting links between my study of Blake and my study of the theory of criticism. At least the question is interesting to me, and so provides the only genuine motive yet discovered for undertaking any research.

Blake is one of the poets who believe that, as Wallace Stevens says, the only subject of poetry is poetry itself, and that the writing of a poem is itself a theory of poetry. He interests a critic because he removes the barriers between poetry and criticism. He defines the greatest poetry as "allegory addressed to the intellectual powers," and defends the practice of not being too explicit on the ground that it "rouzes the faculties to act." His language in his later prophecies is almost deliberately colloquial and "unpoetic," as though he intended his poetry to be also a work of criticism, just as he expected the critic's response to be also a creative one. He understood, in his own way, the principle later stated by Arnold that poetry is a criticism of life, and it was an uncompromising way. For him, the artist demonstrates a certain way of life: his aim is not to be appreciated or admired, but to transfer to others the imaginative habit and energy of his mind. The main work of criticism is teaching, and teaching for Blake cannot be separated from creation.

Blake's statements about art are extreme enough to make it clear that he is demanding some kind of mental adjustment to take them in. One of the Laocoon Aphorisms reads: "A Poet, a Painter, a Musician, an Architect: the Man Or Woman who is not one of these is not a Christian." If we respond to this in terms of what we ordinarily associate with the words used, the aphorism will sound, as Blake intended it to sound, like someone in the last stages of paranoia. Blake has an unusual faculty for putting his central beliefs in this mock-paranoid form, and in consequence has deliberately misled all readers who would rather believe that he was mad than that their own use of language could be inadequate. Thus when a Devil says in *The Marriage of Heaven and Hell:* "those who envy or calumniate great men hate God; for there is no other God," our habitual understanding of the phrase "great men" turns the remark into something that makes Carlyle at his worst sound by comparison like a wise and prudent thinker. When we read in the *Descriptive Catalogue,* however, that Chaucer's Parson is "according to Christ's definition, the greatest of his age," we begin to wonder if this paradoxical Devil has really so sulphurous a smell. Similarly, Blake's equating of the arts with Christianity implies, first, that his conception of art includes much more than we usually associate with it, and, second, that it excludes most of what we do associate with it. Blake is calling a work of art what a more conventional terminology would call a charitable act, while at the same time the painting of, say, Reynolds is for him not bad painting but anti-painting. Whether we agree or sympathize with Blake's attitude, what he says does involve a whole theory of criticism, and this theory we should examine.

One feature of Blake's prophecies which strikes every reader is the gradual elimination, especially in the two later poems *Milton* and *Jerusalem* that form the climax of this part of his work, of anything resembling narrative movement. The following passage occurs in Plate 71 of *Jerusalem:*

> What is Above is Within, for every-thing in Eternity is
> translucent:
> The Circumference is Within, Without is formed the
> Selfish Center,
> And the Circumference still expands going forward to
> Eternity,
> And the Center has Eternal States; these States we now
> explore.

I still have the copy of Blake that I used as an undergraduate, and I see that in the margin beside this passage I have written the words "Something moves, anyhow." But even that was more of an expression of hope than of considered critical judgement. This plotless type of writing has been discussed a good deal by other critics, notably Hugh Kenner and Marshall McLuhan, who call it "mental landscape," and ascribe its invention to the French *symbolistes*. But in Blake we not only have the technique already complete, but an even more thoroughgoing way of presenting it.

If we read *Milton* and *Jerusalem* as Blake intended them to be read, we are not reading them in any conventional sense at all: we are staring at a sequence of plates, most of them with designs. We can see, of course, that a sequence of illustrated plates would be an intolerably cumbersome and inappropriate method of presenting a long poem in which narrative was the main interest.

The long poems of other poets that Blake illustrated, such as Young's *Night Thoughts* and Blair's *Grave,* are meditative poems where, even without Blake's assistance, the reader's attention is expected to drop out of the text every so often and soar, or plunge, whichever metaphor is appropriate, although perhaps wander is even more accurate. No doubt the development of Blake's engraving technique had much to do with the plotlessness of the engraved poems. We notice that the three poems of Blake in which the sense of narrative movement is strongest—*Tiriel, The French Revolution, The Four Zoas*—were never engraved. We notice too that the illustration on a plate often does not illustrate the text on the same plate, and that in one copy of *Jerusalem* the sequence of plates in Part Two is slightly different. The elimination of narrative movement is clearly central to the structure of these poems, and the device of a sequence of plates is consistent with the whole scheme, not a mere accident.

The theme of *Milton* is an instant of illumination in the mind of the poet, an instant which, like the moments of recognition in Proust, links him with a series of previous moments stretching back to the creation of the world. Proust was led to see men as giants in time, but for Blake there is only one giant, Albion, whose dream is time. For Blake in *Milton,* as for Eliot in *Little Gidding,* history is a pattern of timeless moments. What is said, so to speak, in the text of *Milton* is designed to present the context of the illuminated moment as a single simultaneous pattern of apprehension. Hence it does not form a narrative, but recedes spatially, as it were, from that moment. *Jerusalem* is conceived like a painting of the Last Judgement, stretching from heaven to hell and crowded with figures and allusions. Again, everything said in the text is intended to fit somewhere into this simultaneous conceptual pattern, not to form a linear narrative. If I ever get a big enough office, I shall have the hundred plates of my *Jerusalem* reproduction framed and hung around the walls, so that the frontispiece will have the second plate on one side and the last plate on the other. This will be *Jerusalem* presented as Blake thought of it, symbolizing the state of mind in which the poet himself could say: "I see the Past, Present & Future existing all at once Before me." In the still later Job engravings the technique of placing the words within a pictorial unit is of course much more obvious.

Many forms of literature, including the drama, fiction, and epic and narrative poetry, depend on narrative movement in a specific way. That is, they depend for their appeal on the participation of the reader or listener in the narrative as it moves along in time. It is continuity that keeps us turning the pages of a novel, or sitting in a theatre. But there is always something of a summoned-up illusion about such continuity. We may keep reading a novel or attending to a play "to see how it turns out." But once we know how it turns out, and the spell ceases to bind us, we tend to forget the continuity, the very element in the play or novel that enabled us to participate in it. Remembering the plot of anything seems to be unusually difficult. Every member of this audience is familiar with many literary narratives, could even lecture on them with very little notice, and yet could not give a consecutive account of what happened in them, just as all the evangelical zeal of the hero of *The Way of All Flesh* was not equal to remembering the story of the resurrection of Christ in the Gospel of John. Nor does this seem particularly regrettable. Just as the pun is the lowest form of wit, so it is generally agreed, among knowledgeable people like ourselves, that summarizing a plot is the lowest form of criticism.

I have dealt with this question elsewhere, and can only give the main point here. Narrative in literature may also be seen as theme, and theme *is* narrative, but narrative seen as a simultaneous unity. At a certain point in the narrative, the point which Aristotle calls *anagnorisis* or recognition, the sense of linear continuity or participation in the action changes perspective, and what we now see is a total design or unifying structure in the narrative. In detective stories, when we find out who done it, or in certain types of comedy or romance that depend on what are now called "gimmicks," such as Jonson's *Epicoene,* the point of *anagnorisis* is the revelation of something which has previously been a mystery. In such works Aristotle's word *anagnorisis* is best translated "discovery." But in most serious works of literature, and more particularly in epics and tragedies, the better translation is "recognition." The reader already knows what is going to happen, but wishes to see, or rather to participate in, the completion of the design.

Thus the end of reading or listening is the beginning of critical understanding, and nothing that we call criticism can begin until the whole of what it is striving to comprehend has been presented to it. Participation in the continuity of narrative leads to the discovery or recognition of the theme, which *is* the narrative seen as total design. This theme is what, as we say, the story has been all about, the point of telling it. What we reach at the end of participation becomes the center of our critical attention. The elements in the narrative thereupon regroup themselves in a new way. Certain unusually vivid bits of characterization or scenes of exceptional intensity move up near the center of our memory. This reconstructing and regrouping of elements in our critical response to a narrative goes on more or less unconsciously, but the fact that it goes on is what makes remembering plot so difficult.

Thus there are two kinds of response to a work of literature, especially one that tells a story. The first kind is a participating response in time, moving in measure like a dancer with the rhythm of continuity. It is typically an uncritical, or more accurately a pre-critical response. We cannot begin criticism, strictly speaking, until we have heard the author out, unless he is a bore, when the critical response starts prematurely and, as we say, we can't get into the book. The second kind of response is thematic, detached, fully conscious, and one which sees and is capable of examining the work as a simultaneous whole. It may be an act of understanding, or it may be a value-judgement, or it may be both. Naturally these two types of response overlap more in practice than I suggest here, but the distinction between them is clear enough, and fundamental in the theory of criticism. Some critics, including Professors Wimsatt and Beardsley in *The Verbal Icon,* stress the deficiencies of "holism" as a critical theory; but we should distinguish between "holism" as a critical theory and as a heuristic principle.

There are of course great differences of emphasis within literature itself, according to which kind of response the author is more interested in. At one pole of fiction we have the pure storyteller, whose sole interest is in suspense and the pacing of narrative, and who could not care less what the larger meaning of his story was, or what a critic would find in it afterwards. The attitude of such a storyteller is expressed in the well-known preface to *Huckleberry Finn:* "Persons attempting to find a motive in this narrative will be prosecuted; persons attempting to find a moral in it will be banished; persons attempting to find a plot in it will be shot." Motive and moral and plot certainly are in *Huckleberry Finn,* but the author, or so he says, doesn't want to hear about them. All the storyteller wants to do is to keep the attention of his audience to the end: once the end is reached, he has no further interest in his audience. He may even be hostile to criticism or anti-intellectual in his attitude to literature, afraid that criticism will spoil the simple entertainment that he designed. The lyrical poet concerned with expressing certain feelings or emotions in the lyrical conventions of his day often takes a similar attitude, because it is natural for him to identify his conventional literary emotions with his "real" personal emotions. He therefore feels that if the critic finds any meaning or significance in his work beyond the intensity of those emotions, it must be only what the critic wants to say instead. Anti-critical statements are usually designed only to keep the critic in his place, but the attitude they represent, when genuine, is objective, thrown outward into the designing of the continuity. It is the attitude that Schiller, in his essay on *Naive and Sentimental Poetry,* means by naive, and which includes what we mean in English by naive. Naive writers' *obiter dicta* are often repeated, for consolation, by the kind of critic who is beginning to suspect that literary criticism is a more difficult discipline than he realized when he entered into it. But it is not possible for any reader today to respond to a work of literature with complete or genuine naivete. Response is what Schiller calls sentimental by its very nature, and is hence to some degree involved with criticism.

If we compare, let us say, Malory with Spenser, we can see that Malory's chief interest is in telling the stories in the "French book" he is using. He seems to know that some of them, especially the Grail stories, have overtones in them that the reader will linger with long after he has finished reading. But Malory makes no explicit reference to this, nor does one feel that Malory himself, preoccupied as he was with a nervous habit of robbing churches, would have been much interested in a purely critical reaction to his book. But for Spenser it is clear that the romance form, the quest of the knight journeying into a dark forest in search of some sinister villain who can be forced to release some suppliant female, is merely a projection of what Spenser really wants to say. When he says at the end of Book II of *The Faerie Queene:*

> Now gins this goodly frame of Temperaunce
> Fayrely to rise

it is clear that his interest is thematic, in the emergence of a fully articulated view of the virtue of Temperance which the reader can contemplate, as it were, like a statue, seeing all of its parts at once. This simultaneous vision extends over the entire poem, for Temperance is only one of the virtues surrounding the ideal Prince, and the emergence of the total form of that Prince is the thematic mould into which the enormous narrative is finally poured. The stanza in Spenser, especially the final alexandrine, has a role rather similar to the engraved design in Blake: it deliberately arrests the narrative and forces the reader to concentrate on something else.

In our day the prevailing attitude to fiction is overwhelmingly thematic. Even as early as Dickens we often feel that the plot, when it is a matter of unplausible mysteries unconvincingly revealed, is something superimposed on the real narrative, which is more like a procession of characters. In our day the born storyteller is even rather peripheral to fiction, at best a border-line case like Somerset Maugham, and the serious novelist is as a rule the novelist who writes not because he has a story to tell but because he has a theme to illustrate. One reason for this present preference of the thematic is that the ironic tone is central to modern literature. It is the function of irony, typically in Greek tragedy, to give the audience a clearer view of the total design than the actors themselves are aware of. Irony thus sets up a thematic detachment as soon as possible in the work, and provides an additional clue to the total meaning.

There may be, then, and there usually is, a kind of empathic communion set up in the reader or audience of a work of literature, which follows the work continuously to the end. The sense of empathy may be established by a story, where we read on to see what happens. Or by a pulsating rhythm, such as the dactylic hexameter in Homer, which has a surge and sweep that can carry us through even the longueurs referred to by Horace. We notice the effectiveness of rhythm in continuity more clearly in music, and most clearly in fast movements. I recall a cartoon of a tired man at a concert consulting his program and saying: "Well, the next movement is *prestissimo molto ed appassionato,* thank God." Or by the fluctuating intensity of a mood or emotion, again most clearly in music and in lyrical poetry. Or by a continuous sense of lifelikeness in realistic fiction, a sense which can extend itself even to realistic painting, as the eye darts from one detail to another. All these empathic responses are "naive," or essentially pre-critical.

Certain forms of art are also designed to give us the strongest possible emphasis on the continuous process of creation. The sketch, for example, is often more prized than the finished painting because of the greater sense of process in it. *Tachisme* and action-painting, spontaneous improvisation in swing, jazz, or more recently electronic music, and the kind of action-poetry, often read to jazz, which evokes the ghosts of those primeval jam-sessions postulated by early critics of the ballad, are more complete examples. All forms of art which lay great stress on continuous spontaneity seem to have a good deal of resistance to criticism, even to the education which is the natural context of criticism. We are told in Professor Lord's *Singer of Tales* that the most continuous form of poetry ever devised, the formulaic epic, demands illiteracy for success on the part of the poet, and there seems to be an inevitable affinity between the continuous and the unreflecting.

It is this continuity which is particularly Aristotle's imitation of an action. One's attention is completely absorbed in it: no other work of art is demanding attention at the same time, hence one has the sense of a unique and novel experience, at least as an ideal (for of course one may be rereading a book or seeing a familiar play). But, as in the world of action itself, one cannot participate and be a spectator at the same time. At best one is what Wyndham Lewis calls a "dithyrambic spectator." Lewis's disapproval of the dithyrambic spectator indicates an opposed emphasis on the detached contemplation of the entire work of art, and one so extreme that it talks of eliminating the sense of linear participating movement in the arts altogether. It would not clarify our argument to examine Lewis's very muddled polemics at this point, but they have some interest as documents in a tradition which strongly emphasized a visual and contemplative approach to art. Blake's plotless prophecies are, somewhat unexpectedly, in a similar (though by no means identical) tradition.

Just as the sense of participation in the movement of literature is absorbed, unique and novel, isolated from everything else, so the contemplative sense of its simultaneous wholeness tends to put the work of literature in some kind of framework or context. There are several such contexts, some of them indicated already. One of them is the allegorical context, where the total meaning or significance of the literary work is seen in relation to other forms of significance, such as moral ideas or historical events. A few works of literature, such as *The Pilgrim's Progress*, are technically allegories, which means that this explicit relation to external meaning is also a part of its continuity. Most literary works are not allegorical in this technical sense, but they bear a relation to historical events and moral ideas which is brought out in the kind of criticism usually called commentary. As I have explained elsewhere, commentary allegorizes the works it comments on.

We notice that Blake is somewhat ambiguous in his use of the term "allegory." He says in a letter to Butts, "Allegory addressed to the Intellectual powers . . . is My Definition of the Most Sublime Poetry." But in commenting on one of his paintings of the Last Judgement, he says: "The Last Judgment is not Fable or Allegory, but Vision. Fable or Allegory are a totally distinct & inferior kind of Poetry." The first use of the term recognizes the fact that "the most sublime poetry," including his own prophecies, will demand commentary. The second use indicates that his own poems and pictures are not allegorical in the Spenserian or continuous sense, nor are they allegorical in a much more obvious and central way. They do not subordinate their literary qualities to the ideas they convey, on the assumption that the latter are more important. In the second passage quoted above Blake goes on to say with great precision: "Fable is allegory, but what Critics call The Fable, is Vision itself."

Fable is here taken in its eighteenth-century critical sense of fiction or literary structure. Aristotle's word for intellectual content, *dianoia,* "thought," can be understood in two ways, as a moral attached to a fable, or as the structure of the fable itself. The latter, according to Blake, contains its own moral significances by implication, and it destroys its imaginative quality to assume that some external moral attached to it can be a definitive translation of its "thought."

We touch here on a central dilemma of literature. If literature is didactic, it tends to injure its own integrity; if it ceases wholly to be didactic, it tends to injure its own seriousness. "Didactic poetry is my abhorrence," said Shelley, but it is clear that if the main body of Shelley's work had not been directly concerned with social, moral, religious, philosophical, political issues he would have lost most of his self-respect as a poet. Nobody wants to be an ineffectual angel, and Bernard Shaw, one of Shelley's most direct descendants in English literature, insisted that art should never be anything but didactic. This dilemma is partly solved by giving an ironic resolution to a work of fiction. The ironic resolution is the negative pole of the allegorical one. Irony presents a human conflict which, unlike a comedy, a romance, or even a tragedy, is unsatisfactory and incomplete unless we see in it a significance beyond itself, something typical of the human situation as a whole. What that significance is, irony does not say: it leaves that question up to the reader or audience. Irony preserves the seriousness of literature by demanding an expanded perspective on the action it presents, but it preserves the integrity of literature by not limiting or prescribing for that perspective.

Blake is clearly not an ironic writer, however, any more than he is an allegorist, and we must look for some other element in his thematic emphasis. A third context to which the theme of a literary work may be attached is its context in literature itself, or what we may call its archetypal framework. Just as continuous empathy is naive and absorbed in a unique and novel experience, so the contemplation of a unified work is self-conscious, educated, and one which tends to classify its object. We cannot in practice study a literary work without remembering that we have encountered many similar ones previously. Hence after following a narrative through to the end, our critical response includes the establishing of its categories, which are chiefly its convention and its genre. In this perspective the particular story is seen as a *projection* of the theme, as one of an infinite number of possible ways of getting to the theme. What we have just experienced we now see to be a comedy, a tragedy, a courtly love lyrical complaint, or one of innumerable treatments of the Tristan or Endymion or Faust story.

Further, just as some works of literature are explicitly or continuously allegorical, so some works are continuously, or at least explicitly, allusive, calling the reader's attention to their relation to previous works. If we try to consider *Lycidas* in isolation from the tradition of the pastoral elegy established by Theocritus and Virgil, or *Ash Wednesday* in isolation from its relation to Dante's *Purgatorio,* we are simply reading these works out of context, which is as bad a critical procedure as quoting a passage out of context. If we read an Elizabethan sonnet sequence without taking account of the conventional nature of every feature in it, including the poet's protests that he is not following convention and is really in love with a real person, we shall merely substitute the wrong context for the right one. That is, the sonnet sequence will become a biographical allegory, as the sonnets of Shakespeare do when, with Oscar Wilde, we reach the conclusion that the profoundest understanding of these sonnets, the deepest appreciation of all their eloquence and passion and power, comes when we identify the "man in hue" of Sonnet 20 with an unknown Elizabethan pansy named Willie Hughes.

Blake's prophecies are intensely allusive, though nine-tenths of the allusions are to the Bible. "The Old & New Testaments are the Great Code of Art," Blake says, and he thinks of the framework of the Bible, stretching from Creation to Last Judgement and surveying the whole of human history in between, as indicating the framework of the whole of literary experience, and establishing the ultimate context for all works of literature whatever. If the Bible did not exist, at least as a form, it would be necessary for literary critics to invent the same kind of total and definitive verbal structure out of the fragmentary myths and legends and folk tales we have outside it. Such a structure is the first and most indispensable of critical conceptions, the embodiment of the whole of literature as an order of words, as a potentially unified imaginative experience. But although its relation to the Bible takes us well on toward a solution of the thematic emphasis in Blake's illuminated poetry, it does not in itself fully explain that emphasis. If it did, the prophecies would simply be, in the last analysis, Biblical commentaries, and this they are far from being.

Blake's uniqueness as a poet has much to do with his ability to sense the historical significance of his own time. Up to that time, literature and the arts had much the same educational and cultural value that they have now, but they competed with religion, philosophy, and law on what were at best equal and more usually subordinate terms. Consequently when, for example, Renaissance critics spoke of the profundity of poetry, they tended to locate that profundity in its allegorical meaning, the relations that could be established between poetry and ideas, more particularly moral and religious ideas. In the Romantic period, on the other hand, many poets and critics were ready to claim an authority and importance for poetry and the imaginative arts prior to that of other disciplines. When Shelley quotes Tasso on the similarity of the creative work of the poet to the creative work of God, he carries the idea a great deal further than Tasso did. The fact of this change in the Romantic period is familiar,

16

but the trends that made it possible are still not identified with assurance.

My own guess is that the change had something to do with a growing feeling that the origin of human civilization was human too. In traditional Christianity it was not: God planted the garden of Eden and suggested the models for the law, rituals, even the architecture of human civilization. Hence a rational understanding of "nature," which included the understanding of the divine as well as the physical origin of human nature, took precedence over the poetic imagination and supplied a criterion for it. The essential moral ideas fitted into a divine scheme for the redemption of man; we understand the revelation of this scheme rationally; literature forms a series of more indirect parables or emblems of it. Thus poetry could be the companion of camps, as Sidney says: it could kindle an enthusiasm for virtue by providing examples for precepts. The sense of excitement in participating in the action of the heroic narrative of, say, the Iliad was heightened by thinking of the theme or total meaning of the Iliad as an allegory of heroism. Thus, paradoxically, the Renaissance insistence on the allegorical nature of major poetry preserved the naivete of the participating response. We see this principle at work wherever poet and audience are completely in agreement about the moral implications of a poetic theme, as they are, at least theoretically, in a hiss-the-villain melodrama.

Blake was the first and the most radical of the Romantics who identified the creative imagination of the poet with the creative power of God. For Blake God was not a superhuman lawgiver or the mathematical architect of the stars; God was the inspired suffering humanity of Jesus. Everything we call "nature," the physical world around us, is sub-moral, subhuman, sub-imaginative; every act worth performing has as its object the redeeming of this nature into something with a genuinely human, and therefore divine, shape. Hence Blake's poetry is not allegorical but mythopoeic, not obliquely related to a rational understanding of the human situation, the resolution of which is out of human hands, but a product of the creative energy that alone can redeem that situation. Blake forces the reader to concentrate on the meaning of his work, but not didactically in the ordinary sense, because his meaning is his theme, the total simultaneous shape of his poem. The context into which the theme or meaning of the individual poem fits is not the received ideas of our cultural tradition, of which it is or should be an allegory. It is not, or not only, the entire structure of literature as an order of words, as represented by the Bible. It is rather the expanded vision that he calls apocalypse or Last Judgement: the vision of the end and goal of human civilization as the entire universe in the form that human desire wants to see it, as a heaven eternally separated from a hell. What Blake did was closely related to the Romantic movement, and Shelley and Keats at least are mythopoeic poets for reasons not far removed from Blake's.

Since the Romantic movement, there has been a more conservative tendency to deprecate the central place it gave to the creative imagination and to return, or attempt to return, to the older hierarchy. T. S. Eliot is both a familiar and a coherent exponent of this tendency, and he has been followed by Auden, with his Kierkegaardian reinforcements. According to Eliot, it is the function of art, by imposing an order on life, to give us the sense of an order in life, and so to lead us into a state of serenity and reconciliation preparatory to another and superior kind of experience, where "that guide" can lead us no further. The implication is that there is a spiritually existential world above that of art, a world of action and behavior, of which the most direct imitation in this world is not art but the sacramental act. This latter is a form of uncritical or pre-critical religious participation that leads to a genuinely religious contemplation, which for Eliot is a state of heightened consciousness with strong affinities to mysticism. Mysticism is a word which has been applied both to Blake and to St. John of the Cross: in other words it has been rather loosely applied, because these two poets have little in common. It is clear that Eliot's mystical affinities are of the St. John of the Cross type. The function of art, for Eliot, is again of the subordinated or allegorical kind. Its order represents a higher existential order, hence its greatest ambition should be to get beyond itself, pointing to its superior reality with such urgency and clarity that it disappears in that reality. This, however, only happens either in the greatest or the most explicitly religious art: nine-tenths of our literary experience is on the subordinate plane where we are seeing an order in life without worrying too much about the significance of that order. On this plane the naive pre-critical direct experience of participation can still be maintained, as it is in Renaissance critical theory. The Romantics, according to this view, spoil both the form and the fun of poetry by insisting so much on the profundity of the imaginative experience as to make it a kind of portentous *ersatz* religion.

This leads us back to the aphorism of Blake with which we began, where the artist is identified with the Christian. Elsewhere he speaks of "Religion, or Civilized Life such as it is in the Christian Church," and says that poetry, painting and music are "the three Powers in Man of conversing with Paradise, which the flood did not Sweep away." For Blake art is not a substitute for religion, though a great deal of religion as ordinarily conceived is a substitute for art, in that it abuses the mythopoeic faculty by creating fantasies about another world or rationalizing the evils of this one instead of working toward genuine human life. If we describe Blake's conception of art independently of the traditional myth of fall and apocalypse that embodies it, we may say that the poetic activity is fundamentally one of identifying the human with the nonhuman world. This identity is what the poetic metaphor expresses, and the end of the poetic vision is the humanization of reality, "All Human Forms identified," as Blake says at the end of *Jerusalem*. Here we have the basis for a critical theory which puts such central conceptions as myth and metaphor into their proper central place. So far from usurping the function of religion, it keeps literature in the context of human civilization, yet without limiting the infinite variety and range of the poetic imagination. The criteria it suggests are not moral ones, nor are they collections of imposing abstractions like Unity, but the interests, in the widest sense, of mankind itself, or himself, as Blake would prefer to say.

In this conception of art the productive or creative effort is inseparable from the awareness of what it is doing. It is this unity of energy and consciousness that Blake attempts to express by the word "vision." In Blake there is no either–or dialectic where one must be either a detached spectator or a preoccupied actor. Hence there is no division, though there may be a distinction, between the creative power of shaping the form and the critical power of seeing the world it belongs to. Any division instantly makes art barbaric and the knowledge of it pedantic—a bound Orc and a bewildered Urizen, to use Blake's symbols. The vision inspires the act, and the act realizes the vision. This is the most thoroughgoing view of the partnership of creation and criticism in literature I know, but for me, though other views may seem more reasonable and more plausible for a time, it is in the long run the only one that will hold.

KING LEAR AS METAPHOR

L. C. Knights
University of Bristol

I had better begin by saying that I am not altogether happy about the title I have chosen for this paper. "Metaphor," like "myth" and "archetype," is in danger of becoming an incantatory word; and I must confess that if anyone were to ask me for a short definition of "a metaphor," I should find myself hard pressed for an answer. My purpose, however, is not incantation but inquiry, and it seems to me that to apply such knowledge as we have of metaphoric working to *King Lear* may throw light on a problem raised not only by *King Lear* but by all works of literary art.

The problem I have in mind concerns the perpetually renewed meaning of any poem (and the sense I intend would include many works in prose: *Wuthering Heights,* for example, and *The Castle,* and *A Passage to India*). The greater the poem the more obvious it is that the meaning—unlike, say, a theorem in geometry—is not given once and for all, but that it includes the capacity for change and renewal. Harold Goddard, in "A Word to the Reader" which prefaces his fine book, *The Meaning of Shakespeare,* puts well what I have in mind:

That Shakespeare is primarily a poet ought to be so obvious that even to put the thought in words would be banal. That it is not only not banal but is the thing most necessary to emphasize about him at the present time is a comment on the long ascendancy of the historical school of criticism in Shakespeare study. In stressing what Shakespeare meant to the Elizabethan age the historical critics have helped us forget what he might mean to ours. Like the materialists of the nineteenth century, in focus-

ing attention on where things come from they tend to
forget where they are going. They tend to forget that
poetry means creation, and creation is something that
still goes on.[1]

"Poetry," as Goddard says later in the same book, "forever
makes itself over for each generation" (I, 115): and I think it is
plain not only that *King Lear* meant something different to
Dr. Johnson from what it means to Robert Heilman or Wilson
Knight, but that it must mean something different for each
reader, even of the same generation, who has genuinely entered
into the play and made it his own. That is one side of the problem. But it is also true that the meaning of *King Lear* is not
simply subjective, a matter of individual taste or fancy. Con-
fronted by the poem you are certainly not at liberty to read into
it anything you choose. Indeed the whole business of criticism,
of the intelligent discussion of literature, presupposes that there
is sound sense in Matthew Arnold's statement of the function of
criticism, "To see the object as in itself it really is." The only
way to reconcile these apparently contradictory truths it seems
to me, is through an examination of the nature of metaphor
and the metaphoric process.

At this point I propose to invoke the help of Martin Foss in
that difficult but far-reaching and seminal book, *Symbol and
Metaphor in Human Experience*.[2] Foss is concerned not with
literary criticism in any limited sense but with ways of representing life, and therefore of living it. His argument is based on the
distinction between the pursuit of "ends" determined by the will
(and therefore conceived in terms of what is fixed and static)
and the acceptance of a "direction"; between the closed world of

[1] Harold Goddard, *The Meaning of Shakespeare* (Chicago: Phoenix Books,
University of Chicago Press, 1960), I, viii-ix.

[2] Martin Foss, *Symbol and Metaphor in Human Experience* (Princeton:
Princeton University Press, 1949).

the consistent empiricist and the "open" (but not lawless) world of creative living. It is to the former of these two worlds that Foss rather arbitrarily and contrary to most current usage, assigns the symbol. (That for Foss's "symbol" most of us would prefer to use the word "sign" is, for the moment, irrelevant.) The symbol is a fixed representation of the empirical world: "clear, exact and useful" (p. 3), it belongs to the "purposive, constructed environment of the ego with all its deeds and fulfillments" (p. 131). To the symbolic reduction (subsuming manifold variety under a fixed representation) Foss opposes the metaphoric process: "metaphors break up instead of fixing, keep us on the move instead of letting us settle down" (p. 58). Over against the symbolic world of "similarity, comparison and repetition" (p. 89) is "metaphorical life with its seeming contradictions, tensions, and its transcendence" (p. 87). "Metaphor is a process of tension and energy, manifested in the process of language, not in the single word" (p. 61).[3]

It is the idea of process that is important, for what we have to do with is something that goes far beyond the concept of metaphor as an isolated figure of speech in which, as the dictionary says, "a term or phrase is applied to something to which it is not literally applicable in order to suggest a resemblance." It is a process in which terms representing items of our knowledge are brought into relation to each other and to something unknown; and in a mutual interaction (for even the unknown is felt like the tug of a current or tide) fixed meanings are modified or destroyed, and a new apprehension—or (shall we say?) a new direction of awareness—takes place. What Foss is describing is of course *the* creative movement of all literary form, from the

---

[3] For the "tensive" quality of creative metaphor and some criticism of Foss, see Philip Wheelwright, *The Burning Fountain: A Study in the Language of Symbolism* (Bloomington: Indiana University Press, 1954), Chapter VI, and *Metaphor and Reality* (Bloomington: Indiana University Press, 1962).

highest poetry to the humblest expression of an intuitive awareness such as the proverb. Indeed what Foss says of the proverb
will serve as a convenient summary of his thinking about the
metaphoric process in its widest manifestations:

> A proverb may appear as a simile, a comparison, but it is
> very different. The comparison connects one object with
> another in order to procure additional knowledge. But if
> we take a proverb like "Among blind men the one-eyed is
> king," we may consider it as a comparison between two
> groups, the blind and the seeing. If we, however, learn
> only what the simile tells us: that the one-eyed can be com-
> pared to a king when he lives among blind men, then the
> result of our comparison is rather foolish. In fact, neither
> the one-eyed man nor the king is the real interest, neither
> of the two is supposed to profit by the comparison. The
> true significance of the proverb goes far beyond the blind,
> the one-eyed, and the king: it points to a wisdom in regard
> to which the terms of the comparison are only unimportant
> cases of reference. It teaches the relativity and deficiency
> of all worldly power, and this wisdom, without being
> expressly stated, rises above the transient analogy and its
> inadequate formula. It lifts us above these and other cases
> of an arbitrary selection to a lawful necessity. Although
> the form of the proverb is still very much like the simile,
> even like the riddle, witty and surprising, playfully enclos-
> ing a general rule into the nutshell of particular cases,
> nevertheless its transcending character points to the meta-
> phoric sphere. For it may now be stated: the simile and
> the analogy link the unknown to the known, in an expe-
> dient and practical way, closing the problematic entity
> into a familiar pattern. The metaphorical process, on the
> contrary, raises the problem even there where we seemed
> at home and shatters the ground on which we had settled
> down in order to widen our view beyond any limit of a
> special practical use. [pp. 55–56]

The metaphoric process, thus defined, is therefore the central drive of all literary creation (the making of a living image of experience that goes beyond the immediate representation), but more marked and explicit as the work approaches great poetry. There are many works of literature (e.g. realistic novels) where the metaphoric element is comparatively slight. There are others where to ignore or misunderstand the metaphoric working is to be left with but a meagre skeleton of the living experience that is offered in, for example, poetic drama. In a work almost wholly metaphorical a mind unsympathetic to this mode of understanding will be completely baffled and will find, not reason in its most exalted mood, but plain nonsense. A German critic once dismissed *King Lear* as "a nursery story, but of the more horrible sort." But the most eminent representative of this way of mistaking things is Tolstoy, whose remarks on *King Lear,* in the essay, "Shakespeare and the Drama,"[4] may serve to close this introductory section and lead us into some consideration of the play itself.

Tolstoy's conception of the function of art led him to claim that the aim of drama is "to elicit sympathy with what is represented" (p. 353). For this, illusion—"which constitutes the chief condition of art" (p. 336)—is essential, and the context makes plain that what Tolstoy meant by illusion was an imaginative sympathy or identification with the *dramatis personae* as though they were characters in a real-life situation.

> An artistic poetic work, especially a drama, should first of all evoke in reader or spectator the illusion that what the persons represented are living through and experiencing is being lived through and experienced by himself.... However eloquent and profound they may be, speeches put into the mouths of acting characters, if they are super-

[4] Included in the World's Classics volume, *Recollections and Essays,* translated with an Introduction by Aylmer Maude (London: Oxford University Press, 1952). Page references are to this volume.

fluous and do not accord with the situation and the characters, infringe the main condition of dramatic work—the
illusion causing the reader or spectator to experience the
feelings of the persons represented. One may without
infringing the illusion leave much unsaid: the reader
or spectator will himself supply what is needed...; but
to say what is superfluous is like jerking and scattering a
statue made up of small pieces, or taking the lamp out of a
magic lantern...the illusion is lost, and to recreate it is
sometimes impossible. [p. 354]

We may leave on one side for the moment the question of what
is or is not superfluous and who is the best judge of this (for to
determine what is superfluous means that one already has a conception of what is proper): it is plain that what Tolstoy demands
is a straightforward verisimilitude to life. With such a criterion
he has no difficulty in showing (though he does it at some length)
that *King Lear* is arbitrary, unnatural, and ridiculous. Mr.
Wilson Knight, in a valuable paper,[5] claims that Tolstoy's powerful mind was misled by the nineteenth-century commentators on
Shakespeare, with their excessive emphasis on "character":
Tolstoy was perplexed because he expected, and did not find,
in Shakespeare "the novelist's skill, tending more towards 'observation' and 'imitation'" than towards those poetic and symbolic
forms through which Shakespeare bodies forth "a central dynamic idea." Not finding what he had been led to expect, he was
baffled and angry and inclined to shout humbug at those who
admire. What also has to be said (I think it is implied in Mr.
Wilson Knight's analysis) is that Tolstoy seems to think that for
the purpose of critical demonstration a prose paraphrase and
summary will do as well as the original poetry, which is essentially metaphoric.

There is no need to do more than remind you of how far, in

[5] G. Wilson Knight, *Shakespeare and Tolstoy*, The English Association, Pamphlet No. 88 (London: Oxford University Press, 1934).

King Lear, Shakespeare is from concerning himself with naturalistic illusion. Not only are there bold improbabilities (the parallel plots, Edgar's disguises, Dover cliff, etc.), there is an almost complete rejection of verisimilitude in the portrayal of the characters and their setting, of anything that might seem to keep us in close touch with a familiar—or at all events an actual—world. This, as I say, is now commonplace, but a rather obvious contrast may be useful here. The first chapter of Turgenev's novel, *A King Lear of the Steppe*, opens with a long description of the hero, Kharlov:

> Imagine a man of gigantic height. On his huge torso rested, a little aslant and without any sign of a neck, an enormous head; a whole shock of tangled yellow-gray hair rose up from it, starting practically from his ruffled eyebrows themselves. On the broad square of his dove-coloured face there stuck out a big, knobby nose; his tiny little light blue eyes puffed out arrogantly, and his mouth hung open—also tiny, but crooked, chapped, and the same colour as the rest of his face. The voice that came out of this mouth was, though husky, extremely strong and stentorian. Its sound reminded you of the clanking of flat iron bars in a cart on a rough pavement, and Kharlov would talk as if shouting to someone across a wide ravine in a strong wind.[6]

Solidity of specification is the keynote, and Turgenev took great pains to ensure that characters and setting alike should seem to have an historical existence in a particular bit of Russia in the first half of the nineteenth century. "Technical information—for example, the procedures connected with the division of the estate between the two daughters, or the correct names of the beams and rafters in a roof—[he] asked of his friends,

---

[6] Turgenev, *Five Short Novels*, translated and with an Introduction by Franklin Reeve (New York: Bantam Books, 1961), p. 225.

acquaintances, and the steward of his own estate."[7] Much of the success of the story depends on what Mr. Franklin Reeve calls the "accuracy and actualness of the incidents [Turgenev] imagined his characters tied to."

By contrast, what do we know of Lear's appearance, or of what the heath looked like? Lear is a powerful old man, "four score and upward," and the crown of his head ("this thin helm") is covered by a few white hairs; the heath is a desolate place ("For many miles about there's scarce a bush"): that is all we know of the appearance of either. And just as specificness of person and setting is a main feature of Turgenev's novel, so the rejection of it is characteristic of Shakespeare's tragedy.[8] A. C. Bradley rightly speaks of "the vagueness of the scene where the action takes place, and of the movements of the figures which cross this scene; the strange atmosphere, cold and dark, which strikes on us as we enter this scene, enfolding these figures and magnifying their dim outlines like a winter mist."[9] Granville-Barker speaks of "a certain megalithic grandeur . . . that we associate with Greek tragedy."[10]

What this means is that a certain simplification of effect is an essential part of Shakespeare's method in *King Lear*. Ignoring for the moment the important conversation between Gloucester

[7] Translator's Preface to *A King Lear of the Steppe* (see note 6, above), p. 223. The following quotation is from the same source.

[8] On the stage of course the characters "look like" the actors who play their roles, but Shakespeare has provided indications enough that these should be, so far as possible, depersonalized: individualizing gestures and mannerisms should be at all costs avoided.

[9] *Shakespearean Tragedy* (London: Macmillan, 1904), p. 247. Bradley feels the effect of this, even though he curiously complains that it "interferes with dramatic clearness even when the play is read."

[10] H. Granville-Barker, *Prefaces to Shakespeare* (London: Sidgwick and Jackson, 1927–1947), I, 146. Granville-Barker quotes the passage from Bradley when answering the latter's contention that *Lear*, although "Shakespeare's greatest achievement," is "*not* his best play."

and Kent with which the play opens, we see that the first scene turns on a situation reduced to its bare essentials. It is of course the love-test that puts before us the central conflict in Lear— an old man who wants the prerogatives of age, but combined with the privileged treatment appropriate to babyhood; a king who wants power, but without responsibility; a father who wants love, but seeks to treat it as though it were some kind of commodity that could be bought or enforced. Since this sort of thing happens every day, I do not see how anyone can speak of the scene as "unnatural." But obviously it is not presented naturalistically: Granville-Barker speaks of "the almost ritual formality of the first scene," and the formal quality is enforced not only by the starkness with which the issues are presented but by such devices as the use of rhymed couplets (instead of the more "natural" prose or blank verse) at crucial points. Now the "stripping" of character and situation, aided by a certain formality in the presentation, has, as the play develops, a curious effect. Instead of a simple sparseness (as in a morality play like *Everyman*) there is an almost overwhelming richness. Boundaries are firmly drawn: certain interests are excluded, and there are questions we are not allowed to ask. But this simplification is the condition of the greatest possible compression and intensification: character and situation alike take on a symbolic quality and are made to point to a range of experience beyond themselves. And they do this because of the ways in which the reader or spectator is involved in the metaphoric process that constitutes the play.

From the start *King Lear* sets you asking questions, and not only obvious and inescapable ones such as, Why has Lear staged this curious love-test in conjunction with the division of his kingdom? or, Is Cordelia right or wrong in refusing to humour her father? The questions we are made to ask are of a particular kind. Tolstoy sometimes makes it a matter of complaint that Shakespeare leaves us without explanations even when it would

29

be easy to provide them;[11] but that is just where Tolstoy mistakes the nature of Shakespearean drama. The questions raised by *King Lear* do not allow "explanations" that you can complacently store in a pocket of the mind: they seem designed to cause the greatest possible uncertainty, or even bewilderment. Within the areas cleared by a formal simplification they centre on certain words and conceptions: in the first scene, "love" and "nothing" and "unnatural" (shortly to be joined by "Nature"), and then as the play proceeds, "fool" and "need."

Now all of these words are profoundly ambiguous. Let us glance in passing at "nothing," recalling as do so the unexpectedly wise words of Richard II in his dungeon:

> Nor I, nor anyone that but man is,
> With nothing shall be pleased, till he be eased
> With being nothing.

What this says is that no man will be content with mere deprivation until he is dead and so past caring; but simultaneously it has the effect of suggesting that all men are pleased with vanities ("nothings") until they are either physically dead or in some sense dead to the world. It is the same with the "nothing" that plays between Lear and Cordelia.

> *Lear.*   Now, our joy,
>   Although our last, not least; to whose young love
>   The vines of France and milk of Burgundy
>   Strive to be interess'd; what can you say to draw
>   A third more opulent than your sisters? Speak.
> *Cordelia.* Nothing, my lord.
> *Lear.*   Nothing?
> *Cordelia.* Nothing.
> *Lear.*   Nothing will come of nothing: speak again.

[11] See "Shakespeare and the Drama," *Recollections and Essays* (see note 4 above), p. 346.

30

"Nothing": on the one hand mere negation, the absence of what is desired ("Can you make no use of nothing, Nuncle?" "Why, no, boy; nothing can be made out of nothing."); on the other hand, the possession of the inestimable, which the world does not regard.

> Fairest Cordelia, that art most rich, being poor;
> Most choice, forsaken; and most lov'd despis'd!

With these lines Richmond Noble compares *2 Corinthians*, vi.10: "As poor, and yet making many rich: as having nothing, and yet possessing all things."[12]

It is the same with all our key-words, and I should like for a moment to present you with a ridiculously abstract description of their working. (1) The key-words—words to which special attention is directed—are all ambiguous and cover a wide range of meaning. (2) Poetry and situation release and bring into relation and conflict the different meanings: the words, in Empson's phrase, are "complex words."[13] (3) So great is the activation of these words, instance piled on instance in quick succession, that they vibrate in the reader's mind beyond the limits of the specific instances. When within a space easily encompassed by the mind in one act of apprehension we have fire and whirlpool, bog and quagmire, whirlwinds and star-blasting, the web and the pin (cataract), squint-eyes, hare-lip and mildewed wheat, then our sense of natural calamity stretches on and on: behind the whirlpool is all shipwreck, behind the mildewed wheat is all failure

---

[12] Richmond Noble, *Shakespeare's Biblical Knowledge* (London: Society for Promoting Christian Knowledge, 1935), p. 229, quoted by Kenneth Muir in a note to the New Arden edition. The section on Lear's Fool in Miss Enid Welsford's *The Fool: His Social and Literary History* (London: Faber and Faber, 1935) is very relevant at this point.

[13] William Empson, *The Structure of Complex Words* (New York: New Directions, 1951).

of harvest and starvation.[14] (4) Just as there is interplay and tension between the different senses of the key-words, so there is interplay and tension between the different key-words themselves and all the other elements of the drama.

As a way of drawing to a point these observations, let us follow the course of one such key-word, arbitrarily disengaging it from the others. It is not, as it happens, mentioned in the opening scenes where the situation to be elucidated is set forth.[15] But it lies behind both the first scene, where Lear makes his test and divides his kingdom, and the second, where the parallel and intensifying plot is got under way. The word is Justice. Both Lear and Edmund are concerned for some form—a perverted form—of distributive justice. Lear is concerned that reward should be proportioned to merit, that is, the merit of proclaimed love to him ("That we our largest bounty may extend/Where nature doth with merit challenge"); Edmund is concerned with the unfair social discrimination in favour of legitimate sons and the hardships of primogeniture, for both of which he would substitute the criterion of a particular kind of desert: "To each," he seems to say, "according to his ability to get"—"All with me's meet that I can fashion fit." Lear's performance has even something of the appearance of a formal trial, just as trial procedure will appear again when Lear arraigns Goneril and Regan before the Bedlam and the Fool, and when Cornwall acts as accuser, judge and executioner in a summary trial for "treason." Legal or quasi-legal procedure is in fact enacted or referred to a good

---

[14] The effect is analogous to the effect of the sub-plot as described in W. B. Yeats' essay, "The Emotion of Multitude," in *Ideas of Good and Evil, Essays and Introductions* (New York: Macmillan, 1961), pp. 215–16.

[15] "The distinctive Shakespearean structure comes, not so much from the need to compress a series of events within the framework of a play, but rather from a powerful urge to elucidate, and even exhaust, the meaning of the opening situation." L. A. Cormican, "Medieval Idiom in Shakespeare," *Scrutiny*, XVII (Autumn 1950 and March 1951).

many times in the play: Kent is put in the stocks, Poor Tom has been "whipp'd from tithing to tithing, and stock-punished, and imprison'd," and Edgar and Edmund engage in judicial combat; there are references to unfee'd lawyers, summoners, cases in law, beadles, hanging and the rack. All this is sufficient to raise some question about the nature of justice, even without the play's explicit insistence at crucial points.

To the question, What is Justice? the play offers many answers, more or less adequate. The commonest assumption of the characters is that it is some kind of assignment of reward or punishment according to desert, and their human assumptions are often projected onto "the gods."

> Let the great Gods,
> That keep this dreadful pudder o'er our heads,
> Find out their enemies now. Tremble, thou wretch,
> That hast within thee undivulged crimes,
> Unwhipp'd of Justice; hide thee, thou bloody hand,
> Thou perjur'd, and thou simular of virtue
> That art incestuous; caitiff, to pieces shake,
> That under covert and convenient seeming
> Hast practis'd on man's life; close pent-up guilts
> Rive your concealing continents, and cry
> These dreadful summoners grace.

"Unwhipp'd of Justice"; behind that conception of justice lies Lear's own vindictive desire to "punish home" for offenses against himself. Its inadequacy is underlined by the play's two references to legal whipping: the lunatic beggar is "whipp'd from tithing to tithing" simply because he is a vagabond; the prostitute is lashed by the parish beadle whose cruelty is fed by his lust.

Distributive and retributive justice alike assume that man can determine degrees of desert and merit on a calculated scale. What the play tells you is that he can't. There is indeed a justice in the grain of things—something like, I suppose, the Greek *dike*—

33

in the sense that there is an inner logic of events whereby evil consumes itself: Albany's

> This shows you are above,
> You justicers, that these our nether crimes
> So speedily can venge.

But the merely human assignment of guilt and punishment, desert and reward (mixed as this assignment is with unacknowledged and distorting passions), is shown to have no ultimate justification at all: in the play's total vision there seems little difference between the claim of the lawless individualist to assert his own version of nature's law and socially sanctioned legal forms. The *reductio ad absurdum* of Lear's view of his own role as dispenser of justice is of course the mock trial of Goneril and Regan.

Lear. I'll see their trial first. Bring in their evidence. [*To Edgar.*] Thou robed man of justice, take thy place; [*To the Fool.*] And thou, his yoke-fellow of equity, Bench by his side. [*To Kent.*] You are o'th' commission, Sit you too.

Edgar. Let us deal justly....
Purr, the cat is grey.

Lear. Arraign her first; 'tis Goneril. I here take my oath before this honorable assembly, she kick'd the poor King her father.

Fool. Come hither, mistress. Is your name Goneril?

Lear. She cannot deny it.

Fool. Cry you mercy, I took you for a joint-stool.

Lear. And here's another, whose warp'd looks proclaim What store her heart is made on. Stop her there! Arms, arms, sword, fire! Corruption in the place! False justicer, why hast thou let her 'scape?

If I may quote what I have said elsewhere, there is " 'corruption in the place' indeed. Lear's fantasy spins right when, by bringing the trial to an end in mad confusion, it tells him that reality cannot be reached in that way."[16] This, and much else, lies behind Lear's great explicit denunciation—"reason in madness"— of human authority and its legalistic claims.

> *Lear.* What! art mad? A man may see how this world goes
> with no eyes. Look with thine ears: see how yond
> justice rails upon yond simple thief. Hark, in thine
> ear: change places, and, handy-dandy, which is the
> justice, which is the thief? Thou hast seen a farmer's
> dog bark at a beggar?
> *Gloucester.* Ay, Sir.
> *Lear.* And the creature run from the cur? There thou
> might'st behold
> The great image of Authority:
> A dog's obey'd in office.
> Thou rascal beadle, hold thy bloody hand!
> Why dost thou lash that whore? Strip thine own
> back;
> Thou hotly lusts to use her in that kind
> For which thou whipp'st her. The usurer hangs the
> cozener.
> Through tatter'd clothes small vices do appear;
> Robes and furr'd gowns hide all. Plate sin with gold,
> And the strong arm of justice hurtless breaks;
> Arm it in rags, a pigmy's straw does pierce it.
> None does offend, none, I say, none; I'll able 'em.

"None does offend, none, I say, none; I'll able 'em." That last line shares the ambiguity of so many of the pronouncements made in this play. "None does offend" because we are all as bad as each other. That is one sense. But because at more than one point Lear has now admitted his own guilt and involvement, there is a bridge to the second sense: "none does offend" because at the most fundamental level of all no one has a right to con-

[16] L. C. Knights, *Some Shakespearean Themes* (London: Chatto and Windus, 1959), p. 105.

demn. And what is held in tension is not only two senses but two basic attitudes—utter revulsion ("Give me an ounce of civet, good apothecary, To sweeten my imagination"), on the one hand: on the other an unconditional and unquestioning charity, of the kind that had allowed Cordelia to invoke the unpublished virtues of the earth as remedies for "the good man's distress," the good man being of course the erring Lear. Naturally, as we watch or read, we do not debate these alternatives as an abstract issue: we are simply carried forward—alert and engaged—to the immediately succeeding scene where this and other issues are resolved in terms of the awakened imagination.

Lear.	Do not laugh at me;
	For as I am a man, I think this lady
	To be my child Cordelia.
Cordelia.	And so I am, I am.
Lear.	Be your tears wet? Yes, faith. I pray, weep not:
	If you have poison for me, I will drink it.
	I know you do not love me; for your sisters
	Have, as I do remember, done me wrong:
	You have some cause, they have not.
Cordelia.	No cause, no cause.

It is subtly done. Lear's thoughts, as he comes to himself in his daughter's presence, are still on punishment for his sins, on the weighing of retribution against offence. It is with four words that Cordelia brushes aside all forms of proportionate justice and reveals a justice of an utterly different kind. It is, I suppose, what Paul Tillich would call reconciling or transforming justice, which can help a man to become what he is and what his nature most deeply craves.[17] Clearly this raises the whole question of man's nature and the wider "nature" with which he finds himself involved: and indeed within the *Lear* world the line of thought

[17] See Paul Tillich, *Love, Power and Justice* (New York: Oxford University Press, 1954).

we have been following has been developed in the context of these wider questions. Here we will simply notice that within that context the question of Justice has been lifted to a plane transcending that of our everyday conceptions. Not of course that we are left with a new concept. It is simply that in the upward surge of the metaphoric process a new direction for imaginative thought appears. Rooted in the given instance—in the highly complex metaphor that *King Lear* is—it unfolds, and goes on unfolding, in our own lives. In a sense we live the metaphors we have assimilated.

In *The Transformation of Nature in Art* Ananda Coomaraswamy glosses the term *yün* as used by a Chinese writer on aesthetics: "The idea *yün,* of operation or reverberation, is strictly comparable to what is meant by the *dhvani* of Indian rhetoricians, it being only as it were by an echoing in the heart of the hearer that the full meaning of a word (or any other symbol) can be realized." *Dhvani,* he adds, "is literally 'sound,' especially sound like that of thunder or a drum, hence 'resonance' or 'overtone' of meaning"—i.e. the verbal noun "sound*ing,*" rather than the noun "sound."[18] I am ignorant of Chinese and Indian aesthetics, but it seems to me that this comment throws light on the metaphoric process we have been considering. Martin Foss, you will recall, speaks of this as "a process of tension and energy." The tension, as we have seen in *King Lear,* is the apprehension of meanings somehow held in relation to each other, and to a central drive of interest, so that each meaning is more clearly defined in relation to the others, and what I have called the drive of interest is established in a certain direction. The energy is an energy of understanding. It is of course obvious that more than the conceptual understanding is involved; it is only through the reader's imagination responding to the imagi-

---

[18] Ananda Coomaraswamy, *The Transformation of Nature in Art* (New York: Dover Publications, 1957), pp. 187, 198.

nation of the poet (bringing "the whole soul of man into activity") that the work becomes alive. But the point I am making is that the imagination thus conceived is an instrument of knowledge—not "knowledge of" something fixed and definite, but knowledge as a "sounding," "an echoing in the heart of the hearer."

It is in the hope of elucidating this process that I have examined some small part of *King Lear*. The play is not just a symbolic form in which modes of feeling are held before us for contemplation. It is a moving image of life, in the sense not of course that it merely affects our feelings, but that it sets in motion those powers of apprehension through which we simultaneously become aware of, and make, our world.

THE CRITICAL METHOD OF GASTON BACHELARD

Eva M. Kushner

Carleton University (Ottawa)

Gaston Bachelard is best known to the general public of France by the most provocative of his titles: *The Psychoanalysis of Fire.* A wise approach to his method of literary criticism might be for us to reflect upon this title, with its bold linking of a famous method of mental therapy and of the name of a phenomenon of nature which is also the most versatile of all symbols. If we can grasp what Bachelard means by "psychoanalyzing fire," we shall be well on our way to understanding the nature and scope of his contribution to both literary criticism and philosophy through their common boundary: the psychology of imagination.

As a philosopher of science, Bachelard realized very early that an objective approach to such data of common experience as the four traditional elements: earth, water, air, and fire, far from being spontaneous, only arises as the result of a long process of learning. Even the most scientific minds stand in constant need of being reminded that objectivity is not innate, but must be conquered. They are aware that pre-scientific notions are forever lurking beneath each concept, and that "all scientific knowledge must be reconstructed at every moment."[1] The evolution of objective knowledge from its "pre-scientific" state (until the eighteenth century), through the "scientific" phase (comprising the nineteenth century and the beginning of the twentieth), to its culmination in the "new scientific spirit" the rise of which coincides with the thorough reshaping, by the theory of relativity,

---

[1] *La formation de l'esprit scientifique* (Paris: Vrin, 1960), p. 8. The following three quotations are from the same source.

of concepts which had always been accepted as immutable—this evolution is paralleled, according to Bachelard, by that which occurs in the mind of the individual thinker. First comes a "concrete" phase in which "the mind is entertained by ... images of phenomena and leans upon a philosophical literature which glorifies Nature, praising strangely both the unity of the world and the richness of its diversity" (p. 8). This is followed by a "concrete-abstract" stage mainly characterized by the abstracting tendency, the desire to simplify reality by expressing it in geometrical figures which paradoxically enough remain closely bound up with concrete experiences. At last, the really "abstract" phase completes the scientific thinker's detachment from immediate experience, to the extent that the scientific truth may successfully clash with appearances. In the case of the individual thinker, however, the scientific spirit is even harder to conquer and to keep than it has been in the general history of science. For "even in a clear mind, there are zones of darkness, caves in which shadows continue to live. Even in the new man there remain vestiges of the old" (p. 7).

Now the originality of Bachelard's thought comes from his having voluntarily focused his studies upon the initial, prescientific stages of knowledge, rather than upon the perfected scientific state of mind which is that of objective knowledge. Knowledge become objective is knowledge already psychoanalyzed. What challenges Bachelard's attention far more is that knowledge which, having not yet attained objectivity, stands in need of analysis. "For classical psychoanalysis, concerned primarily with the psychology of human relations, i.e. with the individual's psychological reactions determined by his social environment and his family, has not directed its attention towards objective knowledge. ... Our task ... is to bring to light the resistance of epistemological obstacles in the very detail of objective research" (pp. 183–184). It is in his study of these epistemological "obstacles" that Bachelard appears to have stumbled against the fact of their irrepressible creativeness. The pre-scientific consciousness, the unscientific thoughts which are forever threatening the purity of scientific concepts, as well as the poet's invention of images and the daydreaming activity of every man—all these stem from the power of imagination, that is, from a deeply rooted sense of personal involvement in the phenomena of nature. Let us take the example of fire in *La psychanalyse du feu*. Bachelard states that in regard to the nature of fire "the objective attitude never quite materialized; here the primitive seduction is so definitive that it is still distorting the views of the steadiest minds, bringing them back always to the poetic fold where dream replaces thought, where poems conceal theorems. Such is the psychological problem raised by our convictions concerning fire. This problem seems so frankly psychological that I do not hesitate to speak of the psychoanalysis of fire."[2]

But the tracking down of all the psychological seductions which falsify inductions (to adopt Bachelard's own play on words) is not limited to the subject of fire, although Bachelard emphasizes that fire is a privileged phenomenon, the most universally and immediately explanatory of all phenomena. It is change. It is life. In terms of values, it can assume equally well connotations of good and of evil. But other basic symbols such as earth, air, and water may be taken as subjects of similar studies: and this is precisely the task that Bachelard has carried out, following each of these symbols, and their dynamic projections in literature, through the writings of several countries and of several centuries, always seeking the undiscussed underlying connotations of each symbol.

Because they are so richly and diversely endowed with symbolical values, the four elements lend themselves perfectly to what Bachelard calls the "psychoanalysis of objective knowledge." "For the problem is to find the action of unconscious values at the very

² *La psychanalyse du feu* (Paris: Gallimard, 1938), pp. 10–11.

41

basis of empirical and scientific knowledge. We must therefore show the reciprocal light which goes from objective, socialized cognition to subjective, personal cognition and vice versa. In scientific experience, traces of childhood experience can be shown to subsist. Thus we shall be entitled to speak of a *subconscious of the scientific mind,* of the heterogeneous character of certain proofs; and in the study of a particular phenomenon, we shall witness the convergence of convictions formed in the most varied spheres of experience."[3] But it is more and more often in the field of literary expression that Bachelard has been seeking to analyze these unchecked convictions indulged in by pre-scientific thinkers, daydreamers and poets alike.

In what manner can this sort of analysis be related to literary criticism proper? Certainly not by indiscriminate attempts to apply the categories of classical psychoanalysis to literary documents, although this has been done with considerable success in such works as Marie Bonaparte's book on Poe, and although surrealism made history with its application of dream interpretation to literature. Generally speaking, poetry still requires composition, even in the midst of dream transcription and automatic writing. Eluard asserts: "The mere narration of a dream cannot be passed off as a poem. Both are living realities, but while the former is a memory, soon worn and transformed, and an adventure, of the latter, nothing is lost or changeable."[4] Conversely, the therapeutic benefit of automatic writing diminishes in the effort to compose. In short, neither psychoanalysis taken in its traditional sense, nor literature, benefited from the Surrealists' attempts to reduce them to one another. For either clinical exactitude, or the demands of aesthetics, had to be sacrificed in such attempts.

The work of Bachelard brings a new element into the history

[3] *La psychanalyse du feu,* p. 26.
[4] Paul Eluard, *Donner à voir* (Paris: Gallimard, 1939).

of relationships between psychoanalysis and literature, through his philosophical rehabilitation of the concept of psychoanalysis. Psychoanalysis, in his view, is not merely a reduction of dream experiences to a series of common symbols the meaning of which, if once hidden, has by now been popularized; it is a descriptive science the purpose of which is to establish the recurring relationships between the imagery found in the works of individual writers, and the symbols common to all. Imagery is highly selective; its choice is infallibly guided by personality traits, and deeply rooted in concrete experience.

The usefulness of such a method as Bachelard's appears twofold: it provides an instrument for literary research, and contributes at the same time to the knowledge of the psychology of the imagination both in its conscious and unconscious strata. Naturally, the critic who sets out to psychoanalyze a work of literature is limited to texts and documents without the personal contacts which exist in the clinical situation between the analyst and the analyzed. After noting the limitations due to the absence of conversation and direct observation, and to the danger of the analyst becoming arbitrary and subjective if faced with documents alone, E. Fraenkel, a French psychiatrist who has explored the borderland between psychoanalysis and literature, concludes[5] that it is nevertheless plausible to apply psychoanalytical conceptions to literature. He refers to the emotional coloring of the themes usually bound up with a given complex or neurosis. The analyst's intuition can establish links of analogy between the emotional coloring and its corresponding complex or neurosis. This can undoubtedly be achieved quite apart from the clinical situation, in the study of literary texts suitably sidelighted by biographical material regarding their authors. "In a work of literature, the emotional elements accessible to psychoanalysis are

[5] E. Fraenkel, *La psychanalyse au service de la science de la littérature.* "Cahiers de l'Association Internationale des Etudes françaises," No. 7, juin 1955, p. 33. The following two quotations are from the same source.

manifested most of the time in terms of situations (in that a character may be inhibited, or unable to choose between two courses of action, or doomed to failure) or in terms of images dominant in a book or in the entire work of an author, or again of key-words or peculiarities of syntax characteristic of his style. If they often occur in the work of an author in the manner of musical leitmotivs, such situations can serve as indications of the intensity and perseverance with which the author's mind worked upon the corresponding emotional theme. Therefore, we shall gather around a given set of themes the situations, images, elements of discourse and biographical data which are bound up with it and which find their point of convergence in it" (p. 33). In the analysis of literary works, we can, as in the clinical experience of psychoanalysis, base our convictions upon "the convergence of numerous and carefully ascertained details" (p. 35). According to Fraenkel, Bachelard is up to now the greatest single contributor to the field of literary psychoanalysis. He is a hunter of images throughout the field of human experience, but more particularly in its written expression; and he is a classifier of images, with the ability to establish links between images and their hidden emotional contents, and also between personal imagery and collective symbolism.

Now it is a rather delicate matter to speak of method, and particularly of a critical method, in connection with an approach to literature which requires such an intuitive, and at times almost instinctive grasp of the unconscious meanings of images. As an epigraph to one of his latest books, *Poétique de la rêverie,* Bachelard himself quotes the poet Jules Laforgue concerning the uselessness of method: "Method, method, what dost thou want of me? Dost thou not know that I have eaten of the fruit of the unconscious?"[6] In *Poétique de la rêverie* the very mention of

[6] Jules Laforgue, *Moralités légendaires* (Paris: Mercure de France, 1924), p. 24, quoted in *Poétique de la rêverie* (Paris: Presses universitaires de France, 1960), p. 1.

methodology becomes a wager, since the subject of this study may easily suffer distortion if too abrupt a light is cast upon it. However, when the subject is not the daydreaming experience itself, but its literary expression, this evanescence is merely an additional challenge to the interpreter.

Bachelard characterizes his approach as being phenomenological, which means that it emphasizes the image as an entity to be studied in its own right, as *une origine,* to be grasped in its very originality so as to permit us to reap the whole benefit of the intensity with which the imagination has made it alive. This approach is directly opposed to the more usual method of attempting to reduce single phenomena to universal archetypes. With Bachelard, the idea of "originality" retrieves its primitive strength: an image which is original, or one which represents a novel variation upon even the most deeply rooted archetype, is a new beginning, a new phenomenon. As it was created in wonder by the poet's receptiveness to the world, so it must be studied in wonder, as a new creation and a new relationship or event in the Whiteheadian sense by the critic who, through *Einfühlung* with the poet will be enabled to share the poet's wonder in the face of the new vision communicated by the image. Such a phenomenology cannot therefore be described as passive. "The phenomenology of images demands active participation in the creative imagining."[7] The beginning of this active participation on the critic's part occurs when he is able to distinguish images which are alive from those which are not. This, according to Bachelard, is not merely a matter of formal aesthetics. An image does not *become* a cliché by dint of being hackneyed. It is predestined to lose its freshness, its aura of wonder, unless it remains in contact with concrete and substantial experience, unless it retains the physical energy which in Jung's eyes belongs to all archetypes.

For example, all images drawn from the archetypal fund of

---

[7] *Poétique de la rêverie,* p. 4.

childhood experience preserve their suggestive power for the imagination. Bachelard says in *Poétique de la rêverie:* "Every archetype is an opening upon the world, an invitation towards the world. From every such opening there soars a dream of impetus. ... Memories reopen the gates of our dreams. The archetype is there, immutable, unmoved beneath our memory, unmoved beneath our dreams. And when through a dream the archetypal power of childhood has been revived, all the great archetypes of paternal and maternal power resume their potency.... All that is receptive to childhood has the virtue of origins. And the archetypes will always remain powerful originators of images" (pp. 107–108).

However, childhood as a basic archetypal value, as a subject for poetic meditation is more than the sum of our private memories. A new poetic image, i.e. a poetic image that carries within it an archetypal truth, can reawaken in us the universe of childhood. This, in Bachelard's view, is a basic phenomenological fact: childhood as an archetypal value is susceptible of communication for no one is entirely insensitive to it. It brings back the sense of wonder with which a child discovers realities for the first time. Any image, peculiar though it may be, that is marked by the sign of childhood primitivity, has pure phenomenological significance. As Novalis has said: "All wirklicher Anfang ist ein zweiter Moment,"[8] because all real origins refer us back to first experiences. It is the poet's task to recapture what Bachelard calls the "antecedence of being."[9] A poet like Jean Follain, so keenly aware that psychological duration becomes accelerated as we move away from childhood, writes:

> Alors que dans les champs
> de son enfance éternelle

[8] "Any real beginning is a second moment." *Novalis Schriften,* ed. J. Minor (Iena: E. Diederichs, 1907), II, 179, quoted in *Poétique de la rêverie,* p. 97.

[9] *Poétique de la rêverie,* p. 94.

le poète se promène
qui ne veut rien oublier.[10]

Thus faithfulness to origins may well become, according to Bachelard, a testing principle of the authenticity of images.

Another such principle, equally related to archetypal truths, has reference to Jung's description of the psyche as androgynous, consisting both of an "animus" and an "anima", one of which predominates over the other in men and women respectively. Anima is the domain of poetry and of the uncensored language of daydreaming; animus is expressed in the language of clear consciousness and directed activity. "We believe," says Bachelard, "that daydreaming can be the best school of depth psychology."[11] A complete psychology, one which does not reduce the functioning of the psyche to its simplest and lowest denominators, must also take into account the realm of anima, i.e. the ability of the daydreamer or poet to idealize. Bachelard, it must be admitted, has devoted the greater part of his endeavor to the images of the realm of anima as examples of "absolute sublimation." The book entitled *Poétique de la rêverie,* because it deals with the nature of the daydreaming activity and with the relationship of poetic creation with memories which are passive, deals almost entirely with the anima. But animus too is susceptible of literary expression. As an example of this, Bachelard quotes *Histoires sanglantes* by Pierre Jean Jouve, a collection of short stories in which latent, unresolved conflicts manifest intense activity on the part of animus. Bachelard emphasizes that, at any rate, both elements are always at work, in varying combinations, in any writer's intellectual temperament; and that the androgynous nature of the

---

[10] While in the fields of his eternal childhood the poet walks about, wishing to forget nothing." Jean Follain, *Exister* (Paris: Gallimard, 1947), p. 37, quoted in *Poétique de la rêverie,* p. 94.

[11] *Poétique de la rêverie,* p. 49. The following quotation is from the same source.

47

psyche, far from being a mere reflection of the biological division of the sexes which itself has given rise to numerous myths and symbols of the type found in Plato's *Symposium,* is forever creating and projecting novel images. "Masculinity and femininity, when idealized, become values" (p. 73). Their polarity may be taken as a second principle for testing the authenticity of images according to the method of Bachelard. This could be successfully used to explicate the poetic works of such modern French poets as O.-V. de Lubosz-Milosz, Pierre Jean Jouve, Pierre Emmanuel.

In Bachelard's most recent books, *Poétique de la rêverie* and *Poétique de l'espace,* phenomenology is the key word because the author has come to realize more and more clearly the impossibility of applying ready-made categories of aesthetics to the study of poetry: "The philosophy of poetry must recognize that the poetic act has no past, at least no recent past, along which its preparation and advent could be studied."[12] Bachelard even goes so far as to refuse the use of the concept of causation to explain the relationship between a new poetic image and an archetype dormant in the subconscious. He allows the critic no other right but to follow sequences of images according to their own dynamics. This strictly phenomenological approach may be contrasted with that which Bachelard used in his earlier series of five books devoted to the "imagination of matter": *La psychanalyse du feu, L'air et les songes, L'eau et les rêves, La terre et les rêveries du repos,* and *La terre et les rêveries de la volonté.* In this cycle of Bachelard's work, there had been one underlying assumption, clearly and even dogmatically stated, and of which each of these five books constituted a partial demonstration. The assumption was that the literary imagination, as well as the imagination which does not express itself in literary works, can be linked in each individual case with one of the four elements of

[12] *Poétique de l'espace* (Paris: Presses universitaires de France, 1957), p. 1.

ancient philosophy: fire, earth, air, and water, which give rise to four different cosmogonies and characterize four different types of poetic temperament. According to Bachelard, writers intuitively choose their imagery in the element of their primitive, more or less conscious, preference. Bachelard's own predilection goes, he confesses, to the imagery of water. Those who share this predilection "can understand that water also represents *a type of destiny,* and no longer merely the vain destiny of fleeting images, the vain destiny of an unending dream, but an essential destiny which ceaselessly transforms the very substance of being. Henceforward the reader will understand with more sympathetic sorrow one of the characters of Heraclitean philosophy. . . . We cannot tread twice in the same river because in his own depths the human being already partakes of the flowing destiny of water. . . ."[13] Edgar Allan Poe is, according to Bachelard, a poet whose type of imagination exhibits a rare unity the secret of which appears to reside in the deep relationship between images of water and thoughts of death.

Thus, visible throughout the work of Gaston Bachelard is the guiding principle according to which there is nothing arbitrary in the choice of poetic images, since authentic images are always rooted in substantial, concrete experience rather than abstract comparisons.

To criticize effectively the method which I have described, we should have to question its basic assumption, that is, to review the whole matter of the metaphysics of the imagination, in order to decide whether the imagination is as creative a mental activity as Bachelard declares it to be, or whether it is not perhaps largely reproductive, and far more mechanical than he would admit. It would be possible to infer a system of philosophy from the statements scattered throughout Bachelard's more recent work, but this would be irrelevant here, all the more since Bachelard's

---

[13] *L'eau et les rêves* (Paris: Librairie José Corti, 1947), p. 8.

main purpose no longer lies in the direction of systematic philosophy. All his recent studies have been longitudinal ones, pursuing either one family of images, or the poetics of a given form of representation such as space and describing the images phenomenologically, in themselves and in relation to their author. The manner in which Bachelard himself practices this method suggests that he would not demand from others its literal application. He continually emphasizes that he is but a daydreamer about the daydreams of poets. In the final analysis he challenges the would-be critic, not to imitate him, but to launch out on new paths while seeking a similar attitude of affinity, complicity, empathy with a given poet's particular form of imagination. This is not necessarily a vague and wishful approach. Does not any methodology require that the method be adapted to its object? The lesson to be drawn from the work of Bachelard is that the fruit of great imaginations must be dealt with imaginatively. The ideal critic of poetry is capable of recreating the poet's world of symbols. In giving us this ideal, the work of Bachelard may well make us hopeful as to the future of literary criticism, provided critics are willing, as is Bachelard himself, to divest themselves of scientific pretentions while proceeding with the rigor of descriptive science, and to enter into a deep personal relationship with their subject, similar to that between analyst and analyzed, while keeping dialectically alive the quasi impossible alliance of subjectivity and objectivity.

SURREALISM: MYTH AND REALITY

Herbert S. Gershman

University of Missouri

Surrealism, from its origins in the nineteen-twenties, was very clearly oriented towards reality, the here and now. It had rejected the sentimentality of the romantics as being unreal, their formal restrictions as being logically indefensible and an impediment to full expression of inner reality. The Parnassians, the naturalists, the symbolists too, were all, at different times, denounced for having implied that part of reality was all of it, that formalism was a substitute for investigation and experimentation. The surrealists' master in psychology was Freud, not Jung; in politics, Marx and Lenin, not Prudhon or Juarès; in literature, Sade and Lautréamont, not Rousseau or Mallarmé.

Few literary movements, indeed, have been so clearly oriented towards the material world, the world of sense impressions, of human hope and anger and despair, so lacking in a divine or allegorical base. Neither love of God nor blind Fate, neither Muse nor Inspiration, neither Social Justice nor abstract Truth, neither Patriotism nor Family—and certainly not love of Art or Literature—moved the surrealists to write as they did.[1] The goals of the surrealists[2]—which will be discussed shortly—as well as the experimental techniques they proposed to use[3] suggest a

---

[1] The most complete exposition of surrealist doctrine is to be found in Breton's manifestoes. See, for example, André Breton, *Les Manifestes du surréalisme* [1924, 1930, 1942, and "Du surréalisme en ses oeuvres vives," 1953] (Paris: Le Sagittaire, 1955).

[2] I am here thinking of the *members* of the group, specifically Breton, Péret, Soupault (until 1926), Desnos, Prévert, and Queneau (all until 1930), Aragon (until 1932), Dali (until the mid-thirties), and Eluard (until 1938), to mention only the best known, rather than their numerous imitators.

[3] Among the more important of these techniques are to be counted auto-

greater affinity to science than to literature, a greater interest in material reality than in the world of myths. And yet, if ever a group has been myth-oriented it is the surrealists—oriented towards the *creation* of myths, of *new* myths, *for* man and *by* man, and concerning specifically *la condition humaine*.

From its very beginnings surrealism was a movement of liberation, of liberation from the dead hand of the past, and especially (but not exclusively) in literature and art.[4] The "imagination which knows no limits" (p. 14) was the peculiarly human attribute which would enable them to overthrow, or at least shake, the oppressive and smug routine on which their society rested. "I believe," said Breton, "in the future resolution of those two states so contradictory in appearance, which are dream and reality, in a sort of absolute reality, of *surreality,* if one may call it that" (p. 28). Bit by bit we see the elaboration not of a hoax, as is on occasion put forward, but of a myth, as that of the *sorcière* in Breton's *Nadja* or of the *Femme-enfant* in much of Eluard's poetry.

Freedom, total freedom, freedom from both human and divine oppression is a surrealist goal. But man dreams as well as works, thinks as well as sees. If man is to be free then it cannot be purely a physical freedom, but must also encompass that part of man which dreams and is capable of flights of fancy which, for being wild, are nonetheless human. "The mind of the man who dreams is at peace with its environment" (p. 27). It almost seems, on occasion, that the entire surrealist movement, its numerous theoretical positions and even more numerous collections of poetry, stories, and essays, has as its principal purpose the con-

matic writing, the inclusion of dream elements (on occasion dream analysis), and the results of artificially induced hypnotic states.

[4] "Le seul mot de liberté est tout ce qui m'exalte encore" [15], *Manifeste du surréalisme* (1924), in André Breton, *Les Manifestes du surréalisme* (Paris: Le Sagittaire, 1946). The following four quotations are from the same source. The substance of Breton's statement is repeated in one form or another in almost all surrealist texts which deal with the goals of the movement.

quering of the romantic *Ennui*. One must initially be free and sufficiently sensitive, or perhaps sensitized, to perceive ever more clearly the *incredible* which surrounds us, which is the very pattern of our existence, where others see only a mundane reality. For the surrealist there is no *fantastic,* there is only reality, and the stranger it seems the more revealing and valuable it is: "the incredible is always beautiful, anything incredible is beautiful, indeed only the incredible is beautiful" (p. 29).

For over a decade there was little attempt made to utilize this *creative imagination,* the lyric element in man, his myth-making capacity, for the purpose of formulating a new mythology capable of serving as a guide to happiness, to some form of earthly paradise. Between 1925 and 1935 the leaders of the group were sporadically occupied with politics—which left little time for the elaboration of earlier theoretical positions. The earthly paradise during the decade in question was thought to be attainable by essentially political means. But with Breton's "Le Merveilleux contre le mystère"[5] and *L'Amour fou*[6] a new turning becomes manifest. Themes little in evidence since "L'Entrée des médiums" and the "Introduction au discours sur le peu de réalité"[7] are suddenly picked up and developed. Specifically love—not simply love as the high point of life, the physical fusion of dream and reality, but love as a myth, one of the "exalting and incredible myths which will send one and all to lay siege to the unknown."[8]

[5] In *Minotaure,* no. 9 (October, 1936).

[6] (Paris: Gallimard, 1937).

[7] The first in *Littérature,* 1 November, 1922; the second in *Commerce,* Winter, 1924. We might mention in this context Aragon's equally important "Une Vague de rêves," which appeared in *Commerce* (Autumn, 1924) just prior to Breton's study.

[8] *Anthologie des mythes, légendes et contes populaires d'Amérique,* ed. B. Péret (Paris: Albin Michel, 1960), p. 31. Shortly before this statement Péret had noted that poetry and science have a common origin (in man's desire to know) and a common goal (to liberate man by attacking the unkown). The above quotation originally appeared in *La Parole est à Péret* (Mexico, 1943).

The importance of love in literature is too obvious to need illustration; its rejuvenating qualities and socially revolutionary effects are equally obvious, if less often referred to specifically. This *amour fou,* as Breton called it,[9] invariably shatters the daily routine that society has so laboriously set up for the individual, and implies that happiness, the exaltation that gives meaning to life, can be found beyond the frame of family, work, and country. When the Beloved, Poetry, and the Dream are deemed as necessary to life as the air one breathes, then the divinization of love is a *fait accompli.*

This mythology of love is new in two important respects. It differs from the neo-Platonic conception in fixing the idealization on earth, the party loved is of flesh and blood: there is no beyond. On the other hand, it differs from the Stendhalian *amour-passion* in being something more than crystallized passion. The person loved has the attributes of the bride of Saint John of the Cross; she is the *idole,* as Mme Sabatier was to Baudelaire, as Bouton de Chamilly was to the *religieuse portugaise,* Maria Alcaforado. "All myths," said Péret,[10] "reflect man's ambivalence both with regard to the world and with regard to himself. . . . The important element in myths is the striving after happiness which one finds there. . . . In short, they express the feeling that there is a duality in nature, and in man, duality and paradox which he is not likely to resolve in his lifetime" (pp. 19–20). When faced with an example of *amour sublime,* society's initial reaction is normally condemnation, for the two persons involved are capable of any action, however antisocial, in the pursuance of their goal. Religion must of necessity condemn it, for it tends to "diviniser l'être

[9] Péret preferred *amour sublime.* See his *Anthologie de l'Amour sublime* (Paris: Albin Michel, 1956).

[10] This and the following quotation are from *Anthologie de l'Amour sublime.* Breton discusses certain of the social and moral implications of *l'amour sublime* in his *L'Amour fou* (Paris: Gallimard, 1937), pp. 135–137.

humain" (p. 21) and make available to man a happiness in which it has had no part.

Having experienced little but deception in their attempts to *changer la vie* or to *transformer le monde*[11] by militant political means, the surrealists determined upon another approach: rather than follow a political myth not of their own making, they preferred one with deep roots in poetry and the world of dreams, the twin realms of language and desire. That this myth of *l'amour fou* (or *sublime*) has, by the public, often been confused with eroticism is unfortunate. Their common element is their antisocial attitude, and nothing else. *Le merveilleux* and the (almost religious) moral elevation of the one are completely absent from the other.

This conscious myth-making on the part of the surrealists (of which *l'amour sublime* is but one example), this raising of *la femme-enfant* to a position comparable to that held by Mary in the Church, is not without its dangers. The surrealists have long been manifest-happy, and were it not for the quality of related literary productions—the poems of Eluard and Desnos, the stories of Péret and Aragon, the longer works of Breton, Crevel and others—these incurable pattern makers would have left no enduring mark on the intellectual slate. For a while it was not clear that the movement had escaped the creeping monadism that seemed to be overcoming it, that it had not indeed taken refuge in a cloud of bogus mysticism, with talk of magic, intoxicating exuberance and hallucinatory throbbing of misplaced heartstrings. But in the context of the aims of the group, and these have evolved within guidelines that were clear from the very beginning, the myth of *l'amour sublime* is seen as a literary weapon to defend the individual at his most intimate from a society become oppressively addicted to routine and, at the same

---

[11] Rimbaud and Marx, respectively. These two quotations, found in surrealist writings from the very beginning, have the effect of passwords.

time, to offer to society an illusion capable of both revivifying and liberating it.[12]

As with all literary movements since 1820, surrealism owes a great deal to romanticism; but its debt is not direct. While there is, in surrealism, a greater attention paid to the individual *quā* individual than to the individual as representative of a group (the bourgeois, the aristocrat, the miser, the lover), he brings to mind the spritually and socially tormented protagonist of the symbolists more than the love-torn romantic hero. The liberated (or tortured, if one prefers) syntax of the surrealists has no parallel in the 1820's, but it has many in the poetry of Mallarmé and his disciples. The element of mystery, inherent in the surrealist world, where dreams fulfill wishes and words are normally charged with unusual emotional, even erotic, overtones, has only a distant analogy in the romantic wonder at the grandeur of the

---

[12] This revitalization of an almost medieval concept of love, exotic though it may be in our pragmatic world, was not their only concerted effort at myth-making. There is also, for example, the myth of the *poète maudit*. Verlaine had applied the term in 1883 (in *Lutèce*) to those poets whom society had insufficiently recognized, prophets who had gone unheard. From a statement of fact concerning a bare half-dozen poets, the surrealists went on to elaborate the myth of the subversive, the revolutionary writer, who, single-handed (except for the surrealists themselves who regularly act in unison), attacks the society—or that part of it—which limits man's freedom, which prevents the full flowering of his imaginative and creative potential. Hence the rehabilitation of Sade, who had, alone and at the risk of his life, launched a major siege against a hypocritical moral code. This grandiose, Luciferian creature, whose name is now synonymous with evil, is accompanied in the surrealist Pantheon by two other figures, both equally mysterious: Lautréamont and Rimbaud. The former, about whom almost nothing is known, and the latter, whose abandonment of a literary career raised, and still raises, questions of curious cogency concerning the practice of literature, are, both because of the subversive nature of their writings (themes of murder with no subsequent punishment nor remorse, senseless violence, torture, the prodigal son who does *not* return, and so on) and the mystery in their lives, fit companions to Sade.

universe, but does recall the *contes* of Villiers and the *Chants de Maldoror*. So it is that the surrealist penchant for myths, especially that of *l'amour sublime,* has literary (symbolist) forerunners: the utopia of Rimbaud in which woman would take her rightful place next to man, as an equal;[13] the *femmes-enfants* and the *sorcières* of Villiers (e.g. *L'Eve future,* 1886, and *Axel,* 1872); the superhuman traits—beyond man and beyond God—in *Maldoror;* the syntactic and imagistic juggling, as in Mallarmé's *Hérodiade* and *Un coup de dés*—all lay the groundwork, much more than anything in the cubist or dada period, for the surrealist myth-onslaught against society. What the surrealists sought to do was to re-evaluate love, the role of love in society, to put it in its rightful place at the center of life, to make it what it may have been in some distant past: the conscious source and inspiration for all human activity.

[13] L'amour est à réinventor," *Saison en Enfer* (Délires I: Vierge folle, L'Epoux infernal).

APPLICATIONS (I)

The Writer and His Method

MYTH IN THE POETIC CREATION OF AGRIPPA D'AUBIGNÉ

John T. Nothnagle
State University of Iowa

A consideration of the role of myth in the poetry of Agrippa d'Aubigné should at least seem appropriate in view of the almost mythic character and exploits of the man himself. Soldier, poet, lover, violent partisan of the Reformation in France, author of stinging tracts and pamphlets, D'Aubigné immersed himself without restraint in the turbulent world of the late Renaissance. This intensity toward life spilled over into his writings where a vitality of inspiration and an integrity of creation drove him beyond the traditions of his time to produce in *Le Printemps* and *Les Tragiques* some of the most original poetry in literature. To be sure, he was a literary man of his times: a self-proclaimed disciple of Ronsard, steeped in the works of the ancients, nourished on the Bible. Yet, catalogues of sources and influences provided by modern editions and studies only emphasize his vigorous originality. For D'Aubigné, the themes, imagery, and symbols of his literary tradition were the raw material for a body of poetry whose orchestration and tonality were distinctly his own.

The mystery of this poetry is hidden, of course, in the deeper mystery of poetic creation itself where the operative myth can play a decisive role. That myth for D'Aubigné was operative, in the sense that it provided an emotionally and ideologically valid interpretation of reality and could thereby contribute significantly to the poetic creation, is evident from the record of the poetry. The very conditions of his life would indicate that such might be the case. His rootless youth and violent career denied him the educational and intellectual security enjoyed by such contempor-

61

aries as Ronsard, Desportes, Montaigne. With Ronsard, for example, myth was primarily a cultural inheritance from the ancients and served as a decoration in poetry. For D'Aubigné, on the other hand, myth could and did have a personal meaning with distinctive poetic resonance.

An example of D'Aubigné's acceptance and use of myth is found in the story of the woman in white with its many creative effects. He recounts in his autobiography that when he was about seven years old he dreamed of a lady in white who entered his room and embraced him with an icy kiss. As a result, he fell into a coma and suffered from a fever for two weeks.[1] The vision was undoubtedly induced by the nascent fever, but to D'Aubigné it was real and in fact furnished an explanation for the whole experience. It was, in other words, a personal myth that lingered in his mind to play a formative role in his poetic creation. The vision accounts for the personal value that he gives to white which, while it sometimes serves conventionally to symbolize purity, more often evokes the chill and dread that he associated with his own experience. This is particularly true in the love poems to Diane Salviati where the whiteness of her skin and of the moon which her name evoked becomes the emotionally charged sign of his own fear and despair. In *Les Tragiques* the poet's emphasis on the total absence of color in the pale powdered faces of the *mignons* at court and in the bleaching bones of the dead gives proof of the continuing value of white as a symbol of fear and death.

The whole theme of the nocturnal visit recurs throughout the poetry to convey horror by combining the ominous setting of night, the vulnerable solitude of the bed, and the sense of mysterious forces.[2] Of the many examples, the best is probably the

[1] *Sa Vie à ses enfants, Oeuvres complètes,* ed. Réaume et Caussade, 6 vols. (Paris: Alphonse Lemerre, Editeur, 1873–1892), I, 6.

[2] *Le Printemps: Stances et Odes,* ed. Fernand Desonay (Genève: Librairie Droz, et Lille: Librairie Giard, 1952), Nos. I and IV of *Les Stances; Les*

débat in *Les Princes* between Fortune and Virtue where the vitality of the myth renews an archaic form and breathes life into worn-out allegory. The two figures in turn invade the chamber of an idealistic youth who has just arrived at the corrupt Valois court. While the form and content of the passage are conventional, the speeches of Fortune and Virtue have a distinct and original character. But the part that shows the real creative power of D'Aubigné is the vivid evocation of the figures. Fortune appears enveloped in a sinister light and moving with sensuous gestures that accord pictorially with the corrosive speech she makes. The youth is saved by the timely appearance of Virtue who chases Fortune and exhorts the youth to keep his high moral values. The satiric and moralistic purposes of the passage are obvious, but the striking effect is produced by the novel picture of Fortune. She is not at all the blindfolded and impassive goddess of ironic detachment, but an original figure of seductive charm inspired directly by the poet's own childhood hallucination.

A myth of major proportion that figures in *Les Tragiques* is that of the chosen people as derived from the Old Testament. D'Aubigné identifies his fellow Protestants with the ancient Hebrews to assure the legitimacy of his claims and to authorize the prophetic denunciations which he delivers. More interesting than this, however, is the manner in which the myth enters into the very substance of the latter part of the poem to direct it away from the generally satiric inspiration of the first part. To be sure, in *Misères, Princes,* and *La Chambre dorée* he writes movingly and bitterly of the misfortunes of France in the civil wars and of the corruption of monarchy and justice. He contrasts with pathetic or scathing antitheses the present ruin with the harmony and bounty of the past. But by these very contrasts we understand that the essential validity of country and institutions

Tragiques, ed. Armand Garnier et Jean Plattard (Paris: Librairie E. Droz, 1932), *Misères,* 1024–1026, *Princes,* 1171 ff., *Fers,* 1007–1010.

is not impaired, and that solutions by way of virtue are still possible. In the last four cantos, however, the myth of the chosen people invades the poem to govern the poet's thought and color his feelings with the grim vision of tragedy. In the light of the myth D'Aubigné sees the whole universe divided by the intrusion of evil, and all who are not with God are against Him. As a result, nature, the elements, animals, and plants are locked in irreconcilable antitheses. Human institutions are fundamentally vitiated. Men are divided without appeal between the Protestant elect and their adversaries. In these circumstances there is no longer any possibility for compromise or reconciliation. The Protestant *reitres* whom the poet had castigated in the first canto for ravaging the countryside are now blessed as the agents of divine wrath. The elect themselves are governed by the strict and merciless law of a jealous deity who punishes with terrible effect any lapse or surrender. The effect of the myth, then, is to raise the drama of the civil wars to the cosmic struggle between good and evil. In the first cantos the issues of right and wrong were only vaguely defined in the frame of internal strife, and partisan conflict leads only to the pathetic dilemma of maternal France and to the destruction of her sons. In the last cantos, however, the issues are starkly defined. God and Satan appear and the poem soars to the ultimate vision of man's final judgment.

Perhaps the most intriguing myth in D'Aubigné's poetry is that which originates in his discovery of death in love and which grows to inform major portions of his poetry. The discovery itself is a cliché of Petrarchan love, and countless are the Renaissance poets who plaintively await death at the hand of the cruel beloved. However, in D'Aubigné's use of the theme there is a remarkable similarity to the love-death rituals which have come down through the myths of antiquity and which in fact have been observed by anthropologists in our own time.[3] In essence, these

[3] See Joseph Campbell, *The Masks of God: Primitive Mythology* (New York: Viking, 1959), pp. 170–225.

love-death rituals seem to be based on a primitive but valid understanding that in nature life depends intimately on death: plants and animals must die to nourish the living, and the living themselves must pass to make place for their progeny. In the rituals the cycle is compressed so that the discovery of sex and reproduction is made at the cost of death, and among primitive peoples a literal sacrifice of human life was made. It is unlikely that D'Aubigné had any knowledge of such rituals, although he may have been influenced by contemporary folk customs, like those attached to the autumn harvest and the winter solstice, which may have originated in these rituals but which had become mere habit or superstition. On the other hand, some of the great stories of fatal love, like Pyramus and Thisbe, Tristan and Iseut, Calisto and Melibea, may have contributed more directly to his development of the theme. In this respect, Denis de Rougemont's discovery of a Manichean source for the mystique of passion and its quest of death invites further speculation. According to Rougemont, unrequited love in literature is a symbolic initiation by way of suffering and mortification into the pure and infinite life of spirit.[4] From the same dualistic point of view, however, physical or natural love is the ultimate misfortune because it binds the lover closely to the imperfections of flesh. D'Aubigné, who experienced a mystic vision and a *conversion* in the midst of his love affair,[5] was in theory well-prepared to view his plight in dualist terms, and not only to see but to seek death as his punishment for his carnal attachment to the Catholic Diane.

Whatever the source or sources of D'Aubigné's discovery of death in love, it arises from both the experience and the poetry with the compelling realism of an original perception. When he was struck down by an assailant during the affair he made a

---

[4] *Love in the Western World,* trans. Montgomery Belgion (New York: Doubleday, 1957), Book 2.

[5] *Elégie V, Oeuvres complètes,* III, 221.

reckless run back to Diane so that he might die, as he said, in
the arms of his mistress. When he was finally rejected by her, he
became so ill that a physician was summoned from Paris to care
for him lest he die.[6] In the realm of the subconscious the love-
death relationship may owe something to the hallucination of
the woman in white discussed above, for there is an undeniable
resemblance between that figure and Diane whose cold whiteness
first beguiled and then almost destroyed him. Finally, the idea
develops through the internal fiction elaborated in *L'Hécatombe.*
These hundred sonnets are artfully arranged like a miniature
epic which begins *in medias res.* In the first sonnets, we see the
lover suffering the torments and crises of early love in the images
of the storms, the battles between Love and Fortune, and the
conflict of mind and heart. In the next group the poet recalls the
first stage of love with its details and anecdotes, as well as his
first impressions of Diane's charms. The third and longest series
of sonnets records the lover's growing awareness that his love is
not reciprocated, and the anguish and despair that this causes
him. It is at this point that death, which he had alternately
courted and defied in the violent imagery of the earlier sonnets,
emerges as the grim price that the lover must pay for having
loved and lost.

The unity of the theme of death in the sonnets is assured by
the general tone of adventure. For D'Aubigné, love was a danger-
ous undertaking which he approached with high hope of reward
and scorn of risk. He met the challenge of the conquest of Diane
with the gallantry and irrational courage that he so often showed
in life. To be sure, other poets of the time shared this view of
love in their poetry, and figures like Prometheus and Icarus, prototypes of the noble adventurer, appear frequently in the works
of Scève, Ronsard, Desportes, Baïf, and others. But with
D'Aubigné the sense of adventure is more meaningful, for it

[6] *Sa Vie,* p. 21.

defines an attitude that ranges from gay enthusiasm to grim despair in the pursuit of a single objective. In his quest of love D'Aubigné seems to have made a sort of Faustian pact with all that it would connote of exalted hope and bitter cost. Thus the poet, embarked on his adventure, is emotionally committed to whatever results it may bring. When it fails, it brings death.

The myth of death takes form in a new vein of creativity through the identification of Diane Salviati with the goddess Diana. At first this is merely a conventional device to enhance the lover's praise for the chastity and beauty of the lady. However, as he becomes aware that she will reject him, the figure grows to include more primitive aspects of Diana, like the blood-thirsty deity of the Tauri and the dreaded Hecate, queen of the night and of the underworld. It is in the myths and legends of *Diana triformis* that the poet proceeds to find expression for his thought and feeling. Diana the huntress provides the story of Acteon, another innocent youth who was transformed into a stag and torn to death by dogs as punishment for admiring the beauty of the goddess of invincible chastity. Diana of Tauride exacts her tribute, and the lover sacrifices to her his heart and the hundred sonnets to appease her anger, and thereby complete the fiction of the hecatomb. And because this goddess condemned the unhappy dead to wander over the earth for one hundred years without burial, the poetic fiction for the first pieces in *Les Stances* is established. In these long and violent poems the rejected lover flees through the solitude of nature, dead but not dead, seeking the liberation of death, but finding only its *image.*

Hecate, the third aspect of Diana, looses the flood of demonic and magic devices that possess the fugitive lover in his search for death. This goddess of the underworld had traditionally been considered the patroness of witches, haunting the highways and crossroads by night, and striking terror into generations of superstitious folk. That D'Aubigné was familiar with her occult arts is proved by his own testimony in the autobiography and in various letters,[7] and the presence of elements of witchcraft in the first poems of *Les Stances* is unmistakable. The lover is not only seeking death but also seems to bear in his flight the curse of the underworld. At his passage flowers die, birds fall, and blood bubbles from the earth. These are typical effects of demonic influence as reported in a variety of records on the subject: the story of the witch of Thessaly in Lucan's *Pharsalia,* the works of Cornelius Agrippa, and the exposé of Nicholas Rémy. The lover himself practices a form of homeopathic magic as he seeks out the signs and symbols of death: carcasses, fallen leaves, bones. And the macabre chapel that he devises to hold the portrait of Diana is strikingly similar to the treatment of effigies in order to cast spells over chosen victims. The power and the latent horror in these signs and symbols of death add a dimension of evil to D'Aubigné's poetry of love, and open a frightening new world to his poetic creation.

The experience of the self at grips with evil and despair, recorded in *Le Printemps,* serves the poet well in his exploration of the cosmic struggle of good and evil in *Les Tragiques,* and the myths of Diana and Hecate recur frequently to play a creative role. The idea of sacrifice, which was the cornerstone of *L'Hécatombe,* appears in several passages of *Les Tragiques:* in the portraits of Catherine de Medicis (*Misères,* 902–920), of Nero (*Fers,* 977–980), of the princes involved in the St. Bartholomew massacre (*Fers,* 993–994), and of Cain (*Vengeances,* 184). Like the lover who immolated his heart to appease Diana, Catherine sacrifices the flesh of children to Satan, Nero offers the blood of Christians to his gods and to his people's discontent, the princes sacrifice Protestants to expiate their own vices, and Cain murders Abel to appease his own anger. The motivation of sacrifice in each case is different, but the form and consequences are the same. The most fully developed example, and the one which shows the power of the myth to assure an original treatment for

[7] See *Lettre . . .à M. de la Rivière, Oeuvres complètes,* I, 434.

an established story, is that of Cain. D'Aubigné paints him in graphic detail, with gnashing teeth and furrowed brow. He flees after the murder of Abel, but nature reacts in horror at his presence and conspires to make his flight a nightmare of physical and moral terror. This punishment is one of many that D'Aubigné cites as examples of God's vengeance, but it is unique in that the punishment has no relationship to the crime. Instead, the poet tries to show the full burden of divine wrath in body and soul. He dramatizes the curse by projecting it and its effects into Cain's body, gestures, and into the reaction of nature in his presence. The body, discerned for a moment as distinct from the soul, quivers in dread and tries to betray him. Nature recoils in terror or anger at his passage, and reacts in hostile transformations when he stops: leaves, branches, and flowers become daggers, feathers become needles, water becomes poison, etc. The most disturbing effect of Cain's punishment is that it arrests him in a state between life and death: "Vif il ne vescut point, mort il ne mourut pas" (*Veng.*, 200). Exiled from the life of God, he is denied the liberation of death: "Il cerche la mort et n'en trouve que l'image" (*Veng.*, 210). In this D'Aubigné has departed radically from his biblical source where Cain appears solicitous for his life and is marked by God for his protection. For the treatment of Cain, the poet turns to his own earlier poetry where he had portrayed himself, also a fugitive, seeking death in a hostile universe but finding, like Cain, only its *image*. The curse of Diana of Tauride survives in the very different world of religious inspiration.

As the example of Cain and his flight shows, the power of Hecate fills the world of *Les Tragiques* also, providing accessory images of terror for the themes of sacrifice and flight. Like the accursed lover and Cain, Catherine de Medicis and even the damned in hell move through a contorted universe that recoils in revulsion at their presence. Flowers die, streams back up, the sky darkens, and the dread birds of night hover overhead. These devices have entered the world of the religious poem to depict graphically the evil which has now rent the universe.

The recurrence of these myths and of their themes and symbols shows that myth indeed played a creative role in D'Aubigné's poetry. It would be hazardous to assert that they indicate a resurgence of a primitive cosmology in the mind of a man who was, in view of the nature and conditions of his life, somewhat entitled to such an illumination. More plausibly, they may simply represent another contribution to the totality of personal and vicarious experience that formed and colored the inner world of his imagination, the store of mingled and obscure instincts and intuitions that are the crucial factor in poetic creation. When, in the imagination, the inner world of the self confronts and interrogates the raw fact of exterior reality, it is the inner world that exercises the vital powers of interpretation and recreation. In this process the myths of the woman in white, of the chosen people, and of Diana provide a satisfactory means of understanding the phenomena that he witnessed and the emotions that he felt. The nature of these particular myths assures that they will carry an inherent emotional charge because each is intimately responsive to the deepest feelings of the man. The woman in white represents a terrifying psychic experience in the midst of a generally terrifying childhood. The myth of the chosen people embodies his religious convictions and the whole experience of faith. And the cluster of myths and legends derived from Diana, while they may have begun as a conventional Petrarchan device to flatter his beloved, became deeply involved in the whole passionate experience of first love, an experience—we know from the autobiography—that was to haunt the poet long after Diane Salviati's death and his own marriage. Thus these myths, born of experience and rooted in emotion, could and did serve to carry both the interpretation and the emotional reaction of D'Aubigné to the reality of which he writes. In so doing they contribute significantly to the creation of the new reality that is his poetry.

MYTH AS A DEVICE IN THE WORKS OF CHEKHOV

Thomas G. Winner
University of Michigan

Chekhov's writings are rich in literary and mythological echoes and allusions. It is not very fruitful to distinguish materials in Chekhov's works taken from myths in the traditional sense of the word and those drawn from great literary works, because their role in Chekhov's art is similar. We may think of these evocations as archetypes following Northrop Frye's definition of archetype as "a recurrent image . . . a symbol which connects one poem with another and thereby helps to unify and integrate our literary experience."[1] Archetypes in Chekhov's works may be conceived as such symbols in the form of patterns or themes which are drawn from mythology or great literary works capable of evoking ultimate values of a cultural tradition.[2]

An investigation of Chekhov's use and variations of archetypes as understood in the sense just outlined, can contribute to our understanding of the style and meaning of Chekhov's art. Literary and mythic references in Chekhov's works, the meanings of which may be suggestive of total archetypal situations, serve as devices for achieving many-leveled meanings, irony and satire as well as pathos and emotional depth.

Chekhov's use of archetypal patterns may be direct and obvious. Some heroes clearly reflect mythological archetypes. The myth of Narcissus is echoed by *dramatis personae* in

[1] Northrop Frye, *Anatomy of Criticism* (Princeton: Princeton University Press, 1957), p. 99.

[2] See the discussion in David Bidney, *Theoretical Anthropology* (New York: Columbia University Press, 1953), pp. 311–313.

71

Chekhov's *The Princess (Knyaginya)*, *The Duel*, *The Grasshopper (Poprygunya)*, and *The Seagull*. The theme of Lady Macbeth is echoed by Soleny in *The Three Sisters*.

Frequently, however, Chekhov's use of archetypal patterns is more complex. They may be alluded to only indirectly or they may be inverted. Implied archetypal parallels may encourage certain expectations which are not always fulfilled in the development of the *fabula*. The tensions thereby engendered serve to contribute to a tone of irony and to what has been called the curve of Chekhov's stories. The Chekhovian hero who echoes an archetypal hero is often only a weakened version, a pathetic echo, a satire or parody, of his prototype.

Two examples of the use of classical mythology in Chekhov's stories will illustrate this technique. The relationship of Chekhov's Ariadne, in the story of the same name, to the mythic Ariadne, the daughter of King Minos, is expressed by the name of the heroine and by various parallel situations. Both Ariadnes are deserted by their lovers in a distant land. The Ariadne of Greek myth fell in love with Theseus, the slayer of the minotaur, and after Theseus deserted her on Naxos, she became the wife of the god Dionysos. Chekhov's Ariadne, a cold version of her prototype, is obsessed by the desire to conquer. She elopes with an average careerist, Lubkov, and when he deserts her in Italy she finds another lover, Shamokhin, who had worshipped her from afar and who idealizes platonic love. In the end Shamokhin is disillusioned by the scheming Ariadne who is not the mythological personification of spring. Her lovers are also inferior to their mythological prototypes. Lubkov, who deserts Ariadne as had Theseus, is a petty bureaucrat suffering from a speech defect. The puritanical Shamokhin, who dislikes seeing pregnant women, is indeed an inverted echo of Dionysos, the god of fertility and wine.

The relationship of Chekhov's *The Darling (Dushechka)* to

the myth of *Eros and Psyche* has been discussed by Poggioli.[3] Poggioli sees Chekhov's story as a modern version of the myth, "as a furtive hint that even in the profane prose of life there may lie hidden poetry's sacred spark." The ironic implications of the parallel with the myth, however, are not noted by Poggioli. It will be recalled that Apuleius, in the *Golden Ass,* recounts the story of Psyche, loved by the god Eros who appears only at night and forbids her to look upon him. When Psyche breaks the command of Eros and secretly gazes at her lover as he sleeps, the god immediately vanishes. Poggioli notes that Chekhov's heroine, Olenka, is called *dushechka* (an endearing expression similar to "darling,") which is also the diminutive form for *dusha,* or soul. Psyche, the heroine of the myth, is also named after the Greek word for soul. Thus the pet name of Chekhov's heroine, which is the title of his story, hints at the ancient myth. Like Psyche, Chekhov's heroine loves blindly. Unlike Psyche, her curiosity does not compel her to inspect those she loves. Poggioli, in the spirit of Tolstoy's criticism, writes that Olenka realized unconsciously what Psyche failed to understand: that love is blind and must remain so. But is Olenka a wiser version of Psyche, or an ironical reflection of her prototype? The men whom Olenka loves successively—a director of an outdoor theater, a lumberyard owner, and a veterinarian—are but absurd shadows of the god of love. Had she held a light to her lovers, as did Psyche to Eros, Olenka's lovers might also have vanished. It was, however, their prosaic attributes, not their god-like qualities, which could not bear close inspection. Olenka and her lovers are again examples of a lowered version of a myth. The echo of the myth in the characterization of Olenka provides more than a romantic suggestion of the artless wisdom of Olenka's unquestioning love.

[3] References in this paragraph are to Renato Poggioli, *The Phoenix and the Spider* (Cambridge, Mass.: Harvard University Press, 1957), pp. 122, 128–130.

For it also suggests that Chekhov's Olenka, who must retain her illusions, is naive and too simple to see or doubt.

Among the archetypal patterns employed by Chekhov which are of literary origin, those drawn from *Hamlet, Faust* and *Anna Karenina* are of particular importance. Elsewhere I have discussed Chekhov's use of motifs from *Hamlet* in his play *The Seagull*, by which Treplev is identified with Hamlet, Arkadina with Gertrude, and Nina with Ophelia.[4] The casting of Chekhov's characters into situations similar to those of Shakespearean prototypes was shown to act as ironic commentary in which the relationship of *The Seagull* to Shakespeare's tragedy is an inverted one. Treplev, who thinks of himself as Hamlet, is only a pseudo-Hamlet who fails as an artist because of his own mediocrity and not because of a tragic flaw.

The Black Monk (Cherny monakh), in which there can be found Faustian themes, is the story of the scientist Kovrin who is haunted by the delusion that he is an intellectual superman who will lead mankind to immortality and eternal truth. An apparition in the form of the black monk praises Kovrin for his extraordinary intellect, as Mephistopheles praises Faust. Kovrin's fruitless strivings for all-knowledge destroy his wife, just as Faust, driven by Mephistopheles, destroys Margareth. Again, parallels imply an ironic twist. For unlike Faust, Kovrin is a mediocre man who has only masqueraded as an intellectual giant. The pathos of Kovrin, who cannot live without his delusions, is contrasted to the tragedy of Faust, whose intellect forces him to realize the limitations of his knowledge.

Perhaps the most frequently employed literary archetype in Chekhov's works is that of *Anna Karenina,* examples of which appear in at least five stories. In the *Anna Karenina* myth a pas-

[4] Thomas G. Winner, "Chekhov's *Seagull* and Shakespeare's *Hamlet:* A Study of a Dramatic Device," *The American Slavic and East European Review,* XV (1956), 103–111.

sionate woman, unhappily married to a small man, flees her environment and finally perishes as a result of an adulterous liaison with a romantic hero. The five stories in which patterns from *Anna Karenina* are most apparent are: *The Duel* (1891), *Anna on the Neck* (*Anna na shee*, 1895), *Above Love* (*O lyubvi*, 1898), *The Lady with the Pet Dog* (*Dama s sobachkoy*, 1899) and *The Betrothed* (*Nevesta*, 1903), all of which were written after the period in which Chekhov had been briefly attracted to a Tolstoyan philosophy.[5]

The role of the *Anna Karenina* myth in Chekhov's stories is nowhere clearer than in *Anna on the Neck* and *The Lady with the Pet Dog*. Both are stories of adultery in which the adultress bears the first name of Tolstoy's tragic heroine. In both, the line of the story initially parallels that of Tolstoy's novel, then deviates from the prototype. The moral censure implied in the epigraph to *Anna Karenina* ("Vengeance is mine and I shall repay") is replaced in Chekhov's stories by a satirical meaning in *Anna on the Neck*, and by pathos in *The Lady with the Pet Dog*.

In *Anna on the Neck* the young daughter of an impecunious teacher addicted to alcohol, marries a dull, elderly civil servant, Modest Alekseich, in order to help the material position of her family. She fears her husband until her beauty wins her success at a charity ball, bringing about a reversal of Anna's and her husband's roles. Knowing that his career now depends on her, Anna rules her husband and leads a gay, irresponsible life which is an ironical reflection of the life of her prototype.

Modest Alekseich is equally a lowered version of Tolstoy's Karenin. The name and patronymic of Anna Karenina's husband is Aleksey Aleksandrovich, and that of the husband of Chekhov's Anna is Modest Alekseich (the son of Aleksey), which seems to imply a genetic relationship. Modest Alekseich shares, however,

---

[5] See Thomas G. Winner, "Čexov's *Ward No. 6* and Tolstoyan Ethics," *Slavic and East European Journal*, XVII (1959), 321–324.

only in Karenin's negative qualities and not in his limited nobility. Both men are what Modest Alekseich calls "men of rules" and careerists who place their official lives above private concerns. Like Karenin who disapproves of the immoral love affair of Anna's brother Stiva, Modest Alekseich mercilessly criticizes Anna's father for his drunkenness. Also like Karenin, Modest Alekseich speaks platitudinously of life and morality. The stilted double negatives he uses, (*ne mogu ne napomnit'*, literally, "I cannot not remind you"), and such empty phrases as "in proportion to" (*po mere togo*), "in view of the aforesaid" (*vvidu tol'ko chto skazannogo*), recall the affected bureaucratic language of Karenin.[6]

We can also note a relationship between Tolstoy's Count Vronski and Chekhov's Artynov, the lovers of the respective Annas. In *Anna Karenina* the fateful liaison is preceded by a meeting between Anna and Vronski at the Moscow railway station and later by an encounter at a snowy wayside railway stop. Between these two encounters Anna and Vronski meet at a Moscow ball. In Chekhov's story, Anna also meets her future lover at a railway station and their relationship is later sealed at a society ball. But the unattractive Artynov with his protruding eyes and asthma is but a caricature of Vronski, and the relationship between Anna and Artynov is only a superficial reflection of the passions of Anna and Vronski.

The unexpected curve of the story is aided by the literary substructure, the theme of Anna Karenina. As Chekhov's Anna reflects on her marriage, she thinks that her husband and people like him threaten her, "as a terrible power moving on her as a cloud, or as a locomotive ready to crush her." While Tolstoy's Anna was crushed by a train in the suicide caused by the suffering engendered by adultery, Chekhov's Anna does not suffer. Her

[6] See for example Karenin's letter to Anna in which he sets down his rules for her behavior (*Anna Karenina,* Part III, Chapter 14).

husband has no power over her and must humbly accept his new position. The foreboding of Chekhov's Anna concerning the locomotive does not materialize. Instead, in the final scene, Chekhov's Anna is shown gaily riding about town with her lover. Thus the parallels of theme and plot to Tolstoy's novel, which lead to the expectation of tragedy, make the reversal of the story more pointed.

The second of the stories most directly related to *Anna Karenina, The Lady with the Pet Dog,* may be summarized as follows: In a Black Sea resort town Dmitri Gurov, a cynical Don Juan, seeks the friendship of a young married woman, Anna Sergeevna, with whom he hopes to find diversion. When Anna becomes his mistress, Gurov is changed by a love which transcends the limits of an insignificant summer affair.

Here, too, the line of the story parallels that of Tolstoy's novel only to deviate from it in the treatment of the theme and the dénouement. Both Annas take a fateful trip during which a love affair begins, and both quickly become aware of the insignificance of their husbands. The famous scene in which Anna Karenina recognizes the pettiness of Aleksey Aleksandrovich is paralleled in Chekhov's story by the remark of the "lady with the pet dog" to her new lover: "My husband is perhaps an honest and decent man. But he is a lackey. I don't know what he does there in the office. I only know that he is a lackey."

Gurov's behavior recalls that of Count Vronski. At the beginning of their affair, "[Gurov] looked at her intently and suddenly he embraced her and kissed her on the lips, and the moist fragrance of her flowers enveloped him; and immediate he looked around worriedly; had no one seen?" This often repeated gesture becomes a metonymic device which defines Gurov's attitude toward Anna. In the second part of the story, he no longer cares whether he is observed when he kisses her on a staircase in the theater: "two high school boys stood on the landing above them, they were smoking and looking down; but Gurov did not care, he drew Anna Sergeevna to him and began to kiss her face, her cheeks, her hands." In Tolstoy's novel, Vronski also must look around. In the scene before the races, when Anna informs Vronski of her pregnancy, "He wanted to run up to her; but remembering that others might be present, he glanced at the terrace door and blushed, as he blushed always, feeling that he ought to be afraid and that he ought to glance around" (Part II, ch. 22). Later in the same chapter, the gesture is used by Anna herself: "She heard the voice of her son who was returning, and casting her glance rapidly over the terrace, she rose rapidly" (Part II, ch. 22).

The clearest parallels in the two works can be noted in the seduction scenes. The obvious similarities between the characters of Vronski and Gurov make more pointed some contrasts. Unlike Vronski, Gurov appears cynical. When faced with Anna's shame, he takes her unhappiness lightly and eats a watermelon. Similarly, unlike Tolstoy's Anna, Chekhov's Anna becomes quickly reconciled to her new position; her gaiety soon returns and she joins Gurov in laughter.

The Lady with the Pet Dog is a Chekhovian version of the myth of Anna Karenina. Its heroes are little people who lack the glitter and elegance, as well as the extravagancies of feeling, of Tolstoy's protagonists. Gurov is a cynical roué, and later a sincere but sentimental lover, whereas Vronski's feelings for Anna are those of passion. Chekhov's Anna is a simple woman, whose room is cluttered and smells of cheap perfume. Just as Chekhov's two heroes are of a lowered intensity so is the dénouement of the story. Rather than tragedy the final note is of pathos. Muted and transient happiness, the concluding passage suggests, is the fate which awaits Chekhov's lovers.

THE TRANSFORMATION OF BIBLICAL MYTH: MACLEISH'S USE OF THE ADAM AND JOB STORIES

Colin C. Campbell
Principia College

Against the accusation that his Broadway hit, *J. B.*, is a trespass on a sacred biblical monument, Archibald MacLeish defended himself as follows in the *New York Times* for December 7, 1958:

> I have constructed a modern play inside the ancient majesty of the Book of Job much as the Bedouins, thirty years ago, used to build within the towering ruins of Palmyra their shacks of gasoline tins roofed with fallen stones.
>
> The Bedouins had the justification of necessity and I can think of nothing better for myself. When you are dealing with questions too large for you, which, nevertheless, will not leave you alone, you are obliged to house them somewhere—and an old wall helps.[1]

MacLeish has twice used an old wall from the Bible, first in the mid-twenties in a verse drama based on the story of Adam and Eve, and now, just recently, in *J. B.* In this paper I wish to examine what happens when a contemporary playwright with a humanistic cast of mind attempts to lodge his ideas in the accommodations provided by two venerable, thoroughly theistic, biblical myths. I think the examination will reveal that MacLeish has not in fact built within the old walls but has demolished them and built anew.

---

[1] Archibald MacLeish, "About a Trespass on a Monument," *New York Times,* December 7, 1958, section II, p. 5.

79

The deity in the play about Adam[2] bears the curious name Nobodaddy, which is also the play's title, a word borrowed by MacLeish from William Blake who coined it out of "nobody" and "daddy" and employed it as a derisive term for Jehovah.

Act I opens in the Garden. The serpent, depicted here as the voice of Adam's unawakened humanhood, is explaining to him that the God he fears to disobey is no more than the embodiment of the evolutionary energies of nature, a being who cannot undo anything he has done, who created the earth, argues the serpent,

> And set the solemn sun to roll in heaven,
> And now in all things living pushes on
> A muddy purpose to blind burrowing ends
> He cannot see before. [p. 17]

Convinced by the serpent's dialectic, Eve acts on behalf of her hesitant mate and picks the forbidden fruit. She and Adam do not die, as God had threatened they would, but something else almost as decisive occurs—their thinking undergoes a change of base. For the first time they experience self-consciousness and along with it a chilling sense of loneliness, realizing that rebellion has severed their oneness with animal nature.

In Act II, tormented by dread, they flee from the Garden, already perceiving that their awakening to self-awareness from the long animal sleep is going to be a blessing mixed with pain, the pain of being aliens in a universe which does not care about human beings or their values.

The setting for Act III is the desert east of Eden. Thirty-five years have elapsed. The land is in drought, and Abel's flocks and Cain's crops are dying. We see Cain digging in the cracked earth as Abel enters carrying a lamb which he prepares to sacrifice. When Abel announces his intention to pray for permission to return to Eden, his brother cries out against it.

[2] Archibald MacLeish, *Nobodaddy* (Cambridge, Mass.: Dunster House, 1926), p. 17.

> If we bow
> We'll never stand upright on earth again.
> The things that serve him go on knuckle bones
> Turning their backs upon the light. Crawl, crawl,
> Crawl if you love him. On your hands and knees
> Crawl back to Eden. [59]

As Abel performs the sacrifice, Cain recognizes more clearly than before that he and his brother are conflicting aspects of the impulse toward humanhood. He sees that Abel is the thick vein knotting him to the earth's body, and in a frenzy he stabs him with the sacrificial knife. As the play ends, Cain runs off blindly into the darkness.

With even so brief an account of the plot before us as this one, we can see how sharply MacLeish has diverged from the Bible story. God is not the omnipotent, consciously purposive deity of Genesis but the life-force in nature. Adam is not the first sinner but humanity's first hero. Eve is not Satan's dupe but the instrument of man's rebellion against his animal origins. The serpent is not the original liar but the impulse toward freedom. Abel is not Jehovah's favorite but the symbol of humanity's cowardly desire to return to the womb of nature. And Cain is not the first murderer but the heroic figure who dares to cut the cord binding man to the sod, thus completing what his father had begun. On one side we have the story of man's fall from perfection, his loss of immortality, his expulsion from paradise and degeneration into fratricide, and on the other the story of man's insurrection against his biological beginnings, and of his first steps in the journey toward full humanhood. One records man's fall from divinity, the other his rise from animality.

I think it is clear that MacLeish has worked outside his source, not in and through it. In fact, it almost seems as though his play is a reversal of the Bible story, as if he had taken the biblical wall and struck it down, stone by stone, in order to have building materials for one of his own.

81

Let us turn now to *J. B.*[3] The problem which propels it came alive in MacLeish's thinking when he was in London during World War II just after the blitz. The slaughter of civilians in the Luftwaffe bombings disturbed him profoundly, and the more he ruminated on the senselessness of much human suffering the closer his thinking was driven toward the classic treatment of this question in western literature, toward the Book of Job, where he found another old wall very much to his liking.

The setting is a circus tent with a raised platform to one side. The action commences with the entrance of Zuss and Nickles, two unemployed actors reduced to vending balloons and popcorn for a living. The platform, which Zuss mounts, turns out to be "heaven" in a play about Job performed daily by the circus people. Rummaging about, Zuss finds the masks they use. He takes the Godmask for himself, offers Nickles the one worn by Satan, and in jest they begin to act their parts. The masks, however, begin speaking with voices of their own. Majestically the Godmask intones the biblical phrases which state the famous wager, the voice of Satan accepts, and in one of the circus rings to the right of the platform another play comes into being. We see J. B., a wealthy American industrialist, seated at Thanksgiving Dinner with his wife, Sarah, and their children. A mild argument is in progress over the question of God's participation in human concerns. Sarah feels that the good things of this life come from God as rewards for obedience to his will. Her husband regards success and wealth and happiness as things which are just there, like mountains and grass and fresh air. One does not acquire them by being deserving.

This notion of J. B.'s has, of course, a corollary, for if well-being is not a reward, neither is suffering a punishment, and a good part of the rest of the play is given over to dramatizing this,

[3] Archibald MacLeish, *J. B.: A Play in Verse* (Boston: Houghton Mifflin, 1958).

to enacting the idea that evil impinges upon our lives in a manner which is unpredictable and aimless. Savage calamities destroy J. B.'s children and his wealth, so that by scene eight he has nothing left but his wife, and she deserts him when he refuses to join her in cursing God for his injustice.

The comforters come and go, and are followed by the Whirlwind. When Zuss and Nickles debate the significance of the Whirlwind's oration, we discover that the emphasis in this encounter has been shifted by MacLeish from the splendor of God and his creation to the splendor of man in accepting and loving this creation as it is, accepting both its happiness and its pain and loving it enough to want to go on dwelling in it regardless. "In spite of everything he'd suffered," Zuss says to Nickles,

> In spite of all he'd lost and loved
> *He* understood and he forgave it!...[p. 139]

Here we have the play's central meaning. In forgiving God for making such a world, J. B. asserts his determination to remain human in the midst of inhuman evil. He has learned that justice, at least as human beings understand it, is not to be expected from God, but suffering has also taught him that this lack of justice, this basic darkness in the universe, can be partially counteracted through love, a love which includes the forgiveness of God and the affirmation of life.

The attempt to house concepts such as these inside the walls of an old story encrusted with millennia of orthodox theistic significance is a bold one, and we must ask now if MacLeish has actually or only apparently succeeded in doing it.

The play's thesis is comprised of two assertions: that God's creation does not include justice, and that we ought to forgive him for this fact.

There is a sense in which the first of these may be said to be resident in the Bible story, for in the Prologue it is affirmed three times that Job is a perfect and an upright man, yet despite this God permits him to be submerged in brutal affliction. This suggests that the world projected in the Book of Job contains a system of rewards and punishments so capricious in its operation that one can hardly view it as a world governed by justice.

The second proposition is also present, but not as clearly as the other. MacLeish infers it from what happens at the end of the biblical account, where we read that Job rears another family, acquires even greater wealth, and in general picks up again the successful life which calamity had forced him to drop. This is taken to mean that he loves life in spite of what it is, in spite of its blind, stumbling malice toward him, and that in loving it he is forgiving the God who made it. The story of Job, MacLeish has remarked,

> is a *human* triumph. Its answer is not a dogma but an act—Job's *act*, Job's *doing*, Job's picking up his life again. And the myth of Job is a myth for our time because this is our answer also: the answer that moves so many of us who, without the formal beliefs that supported our ancestors, nevertheless pick up our lives again after these vast disasters and go on—go on *as men*.[4]

This humanistic view of the Book of Job, emphasizing as it does, not the core of the story, but its brief Epilogue, will to some seem rather strained, but nonetheless it would appear that MacLeish has successfully built within the ancient walls, not inserting his thesis from the outside but discovering it on the inside. However, when we probe beneath the two propositions which comprise the thesis, and ask what sort of God it is that J. B. forgives and why this God cannot be expected to behave justly toward man, we find that at a deeper level the Biblical original has undergone some far-reaching alterations.

[4] Archibald MacLeish, "Remarks on *J. B.*," *Theatre Arts*, XLIII (April, 1959), 62.

A great many readers and viewers have assumed, quite under-standably, that the God of *J. B.* is the God of the Book of Job. Nickles says that he is several times, and at least once calls him "Jahveh." The use of long verbatim excerpts from the Bible strengthens the feeling, and there is no outlandish name such as Nobodaddy to warn us otherwise. Yet an examination of some of the passages in which God's attributes are expounded will show that the deity in MacLeish's play is not the God of the Old Testament as he appears in the Book of Job.

The Godmask which Zuss puts on is pictured in the stage directions as a *"huge white, blank, beautiful, expressionless mask with eyes lidded like the eyes of the mask in Michelangelo's Night"* (p. 16). Nickles pokes fun at it.

> It's His.
> I've known that face before. I've seen it.
> They find it under bark of marble
> Deep within the rinds of stone:
> God the Creator . . . (*nastily*) of the animals!

This prompts the following exchange:

Mr. Zuss: God of
          Everything that is or can!
Nickles: Is or can—but cannot know.
Mr. Zuss: There is nothing those closed eyes
          Have not known and seen.
Nickles: Except
          To know they see: to know they've seen it.
          Lions and dolphins have such eyes.
          They know the way the wild geese know—
          Those pin-point travelers who go home
          To Labradors they never meant to,
          Unwinding the will of the world like string. [pp. 16–17]

This deity begins to look like Nobodaddy, an instinctual, unself-conscious energy principle of some sort.

Nickles' mask is *"open-eyed where the other was lidded. The eyes, though wrinkled with laughter, seem to stare and the mouth is drawn down in agonized disgust"* (p. 18). Satan possesses what God does not, self-awareness. Nickles recognizes this when he first dons the mask. "Those eyes *see,*" he exclaims,

> They see the *world.* They do. They see it.
> From going to and fro in the earth,
> From walking up and down, they see it.
> I know what Hell is now—to *see.*
> Consciousness of consciousness . . . [p. 22]

Another relevant passage is one in which Zuss describes God as the

> Enormous pattern of the steep of stars,
> Minute perfection of the frozen crystal,
> Inimitable architecture of the slow,
> Cold, silent, ignorant sea-snail:
> The unimaginable will of stone:
> Infinite mind in midge of matter! [pp. 47–48]

It is not that God created the stars in their patterns and the crystals in their frozen perfection, but that he *is* those things, and that he is also the will of the stone, an infinite mind—albeit one dimly aware of itself—in matter, a being who, again much like Nobodaddy, is diffused throughout the material cosmos.

Now, how does this God differ from Jehovah of the Old Testament? Despite the largeness and complexity of the Jewish-Christian concept of God, it seems to me that within that complexity, agreement could be had on at least two properties as being indispensable to any description of the God of the Bible. Omniscience is the first of these, and omniscience implies self-consciousness. Yet that is precisely what the God of *J. B.* lacks, and this lack is MacLeish's explanation of why man cannot expect justice from his creator. The actions of one who does not know what he is doing are neither just nor unjust, good nor bad, which is what J. B. suspects about God in scene one and knows with certainty at the end of the play. Well-being is not a reward from him nor is suffering a punishment. In a sense we have here a view close to that expressed in *Nobodaddy*. God creates man only to have man, by evolution, develop a quality which his creator does not exhibit, self-knowledge, and it is this quality which lies back of man's moral sense and his unanswered cry for justice.

The second property, transcendence, is a much more controversial one. Yet forty centuries of worship by Jews and Christians have produced a concept of God various enough to contain the entire spectrum of warring opinions. One can subscribe to immanence or transcendence or a combination of both and remain within the pale, but when it is asserted that God's face may be found in the "rinds of stone" and that he is identical with the architecture of the snail, we recognize that immanence has been carried up to and across the boundary it shares with pantheism, and pantheism, most of the parties to the controversy would agree, is outside the theological reference-frame of the Book of Job and of the Bible as a whole.

Since the nature of God is the pre-condition which lies back of everything in the Book of Job, including the two ideas which became the thesis of *J. B.*, the modifications in his character just analyzed are crucial. By depriving God of self-consciousness and transcendence, thereby making him ignorant of his own behavior and indistinguishable, qualitatively, from his creation, MacLeish has instituted changes in his nature forceful enough to push *J. B.* outside the walls of its Biblical source.

Myths as rich and orchestral as the Adam and Job stories will certainly bear a variety of interpretations, but their pliability is not without limit. Plot, setting, character, and the insights into human nature and destiny which they are understood to reveal will sustain a large amount of bending. Still, they can be bent out of shape. There is a point at which the playwright using them stops interpreting an old story and begins to compose a new one of his own. I think MacLeish has reached and passed this point in both *Nobodaddy* and *J. B.* Under his bending, Adam, Job, and Jehovah lose their identity. They are transformed right out of themselves.

This transformation, when we consider the man-centered focus of MacLeish's thinking and the God-centered focus of the myths, was probably unavoidable. The old walls in Eden and in the land of Uz will no doubt lend themselves to many uses, but one thing they cannot do is provide friendly lodging for the ideas of a thorough-going humanist.

THE SYMBOLISM OF *GESTUS* IN BRECHT'S DRAMA

Robert L. Hiller

University of Chicago

In discussing the symbolism of *gestus* in Brecht's drama, it is first necessary to define what I mean by *gestus*. First of all it cannot be satisfactorily translated into English as "gesture." It might be translated as "non-verbal expression"; it must be understood, however, that it may or may not be a part of verbal expression, may or may not accompany speech or be acted out concurrently with speech. One might, then, say that *gestus* or "non-verbal expression" is part of the mimesis of any play as it appears on the stage. The *gestus* in this instance would then be the single stone, so to speak, in the whole mosaic of non-verbal representation which the actor offers to the audience. Some of this mimesis may be initiated by the actor as his own interpretation of what the author says. Some of it is ordered specifically by the author, either through the implications of the dialogue or through actual stage directions. There are therefore two classes of *gestus*. We might call these classes "actor-initiated" *gestus* and "author-ordered" *gestus*. The second class, the "author-ordered" *gestus,* is, however, not merely a part of mimesis. It is also the attitude which the character assumes, accompanied and underlined by speech or not as prescribed by the author himself. *Gestus* or non-verbal expression here would actually be the manner in which a character conveys his intent or emotion. However, it may be not only an attitude; the very manner in which a character acts may also be an integral part of the entire action of the play.[1]

[1] This is in fact the way in which Brecht himself seems to have regarded *gestus*. Cf. John Willett, *The Theatre of Bertolt Brecht* (New York: New Directions, 1959), p. 174 f.

The important point, in this instance, is that this second kind of *gestus* is an indispensable commentary on the character himself and on his personal non-verbal response to the other characters and to the events which occur around him as conceived by the author.

It therefore does not indicate only that which the character wishes to do or might do, and it is not merely an embryonic or aborted action, such as a clenched fist, for instance. In so far as it reveals the character's emotions, strengths, and weaknesses, either actively or passively, it resembles in its completeness an action itself.

It is this second class of non-verbal expression to which I refer when I speak of *gestus* in Brecht's drama. This is not an easy task, since Brecht's method of producing a drama did not consist only in the writing, but also in the direction of it. It was his firmly established practice to rewrite whole scenes during rehearsals, not relying solely on his own dramatic judgment but freely incorporating suggestions made by the cast, or even to rewrite scenes after the reaction of the audience had shown him that he had not made the point he wished to make. One might even maintain that until Brecht's death none of his plays had achieved their final form.[2] Of course this is to a certain extent true of most dramatists; but the consistency with which Brecht worked in this respect, and the great reluctance he showed to let any play of his reach absolute finality is particularly significant. The flux and life, development and change to which every drama is subject through the varying interpretations given it by directors, actors, critics, audiences, and the natural erosion or change produced by time itself are not points which should be considered here.

A discussion of the often treated *Verfremdungseffekt*[3] is like-

[2] Willett, p. 157.
[3] Willett, pp. 179–181.

wise neither desirable nor necessary in the examination of Brecht's use of *gestus*. The estrangement of the audience produced by the manner in which the author makes his statement or forces his characters to act is of course actually nothing new and in no way Brecht's special province. Every writer uses the V-effect when he shows aspects of our world and human nature to his audience in a manner which is startlingly new. When Brecht says, in his often-quoted example, that he wishes to force the audience to look at the world and particuraly relationships between men with the "estranged" eye with which Newton looked at the falling apple or Galileo at the swinging chandelier, he is not really doing anything different from any other artist. Therefore, in a discussion of *gestus* in Brecht's drama, reference to the V-effect can only be confusing.

Let us begin by categorizing some of the most obvious kinds of non-verbal expression in Brecht's works, using as our standard the second definition given: "*gestus* as commentary on the character himself and as his response to other characters and to the events that occur around him, as prescribed by the author."

There is, for instance, the "didactic" *gestus* which is entirely in keeping with the didactic purpose of the play and which underlines what is also expressed in words.

This is seen, for instance, in the play, *Die Rundköpfe und die Spitzköpfe,* when the farm tenant, Callas, and his daughter, Nanna, in the final scene of the play, sit on the floor and eat their soup at the feet of the viceroy and his rich guests.[4] Callas, as an exploited peasant, had originally been one of the leaders in the rebellion of the tenants against the all-powerful landlords. This rebellion was broken by Iberin, the popular leader of the reform party, by dividing the country into two races, the nativeborn, honorable, decent, moral "Rundköpfe" and the foreign, immoral, dastardly "Spitzköpfe," (an analogy, of course, to Hitler,

---

[4] Bertolt Brecht, *Stücke VI* (Berlin: Suhrkamp Verlag, 1957), p. 207.

the Aryan superrace, and the Jews). But through the support
which the landlords give to Iberin, the final outcome is a division
not according to race but once again a division into the haves
and have-nots. Callas' humbly eating his soup at the feet of the
great and powerful demonstrates his weak and immoral agreement with this division of mankind into rich and poor. Callas,
the poor tenant, is ruled only by his belly. Iberin's storm-trooper
followers, the Huas, tell him:

"Iss nur deine Suppe, Callas, rühr nicht lange drin rum.
Du warst immer schlauer als die und darum
Hast du es ja auch jetzt zu was gebracht
Und issest deine Suppe auf die Nacht." [p. 207]
("Come on, eat your soup, Callas, don't keep stirring it.
You've always been smarter than the others and that's why
You've gotten somewhere now
And are having soup for dinner.")

While Callas eats the soup handed to him by the great, his
former companions in the rebellion are being led in the background to the gallows, illustrating the thesis stated by the author
in the prologue:

"Es ist der Unterschied zwischen arm und reich.
Und ich denke, wir werden so verbleiben
Ich werde euch ein Gleichnis schreiben
In dem beweis ich es jedermann
Es kommt nur auf diesen Unterschied an." [p. 9]
("It is the difference between poor and rich.
And, I think, we'll stay that way
I'll tell you a parable
In which I'll prove to everyone
That this is the only difference which matters.")

There is another *gestus* which is harder to explain. In the
same play de Guzman, one of the landlords, a Spitzkopf (in other
words, a member of the inferior race), has been arrested by

Iberin's storm troopers, the "Huas," and dragged off to prison. De Guzman has all the characteristics of a member of the rich class, as portrayed by Brecht. He is hardhearted, cowardly, soft, and immoral. His tenants are starving and he has seduced the daughter of his tenant, Callas, and started her on the primrose path. In the fourth scene depicting the trial of de Guzman as a "Spitzkopf," the "Huas" throw dice for the rings of the accused (p 64). What is Brecht's purpose in using this picture in this connection? Of course, one is reminded immediately of the Roman soldiers throwing dice for the seamless coat of Christ, and knowing the character of de Guzman, this *gestus* of the "Huas" seems ambiguous and singularly inappropriate.

We know that it is Brecht's purpose to show that the rich in the end win out, regardless of race or creed. Why then should he apparently attempt to win sympathy for this extremely unattractive representative of that class which he wants us to condemn? Or is this the atheist's crude commentary on the age-old symbolism of religion and church? Is it bitter ridicule of the propensity of the rich to hide their sins and their true nature behind the image of the saint and even the martyr; in fact, more than that, to invest themselves with symbols which clearly put them and their order of the world on the side of God.

Another point, however, becomes clear by this dice game of the "Huas." It is the following: In the trial, although it is held under the pretext of trying a member of an inferior race for the rape of a member of the master race, the real issue is money. The "Huas," who, as followers of Iberin, are the proponents of the theory of racial superiority, show by their dice game that their true interest too is money. Perhaps the ballad sung during this same scene can throw light on Brecht's intention. This is "Die Ballade vom Knopfwurf." A button is torn off and tossed in the air to decide a question, such as, whether a girl loves a man or not.

"Lass uns, Freund, das Schicksal fragen!
Wollen sehn:
Wenn die Löcher aufwärts schauen
Kannst du ihr vielleicht nicht trauen
Und musst ein Haus weitergehn.
Lass mich sehen, ob du ohne Glück bist!
Und ich werf den Knopf und sag: Du bist es.
Sagen sie dann: aber diese Löcher
Gehn doch durch! Dann sage ich: So ist es." [p. 89]
("Friend, let's ask fate!
Let's see:
If the holes point upward
Then perhaps you can't trust her
And will have to go on to the next house.
Let me see whether you have no luck!
And I throw the button and say: You don't.
If then they say: but these holes
Go all the way through! Then I say: That's the way it is.")

In other words in a game against fate man cannot win since the game is played with a two-headed coin. However Brecht qualifies this, for in the ballad the questioners of fate are "ein krummer Mann," "ein dummer Mann," and finally and inevitably "ein armer Mann" but never "ein reicher Mann." Thus one might suppose that the "Huas" too, even though they gamble for the rings of a rich "Spitzkopf," will be eventually betrayed by fate.

Yet there is another point which cannot be overlooked. De Guzman is a "Spitzkopf," and it is for this reason that brutality as represented by the "Huas" gains power over him. Does Brecht mean also to say that the oppressed and flayed human being, whatever his character, race, creed, and even origin, has a justified claim on our pity, perhaps even a terrible majesty of his own? He may well have meant something like this. However, he seems to weaken his point when in the end he divides both

"Rundköpfe" and "Spitzköpfe" not according to race, but into haves and have-nots.

This type of non-verbal expression might be termed the "shock" *gestus*. Together with the "didactic" *gestus*, it is most commonly found in Brecht. In their nature they show the same ambivalence and have the same disillusioning impact as Brecht's language.

We find a variation of this type of *gestus* in *Herr Puntila und sein Knecht*.[5] Here the tone is not quite as angry, for it is somewhat lightened by the absurdity of the situation, in which a tyrannical landowner, "Herr Puntila," shows humanly decent feelings only when he is drunk. Puntila when sober is the perfect Marxist portrait of a capitalist scoundrel, but when drunk he displays such charm and decency that his servant Matti earnestly states: "... wenn er besoffen ist, möcht ich nicht, dass er mich verachtet" (p. 36). ("I don't like to have him despise me when he's drunk.") Puntila's contradictory behavior, gives this play a special ambivalence. Life itself becomes problematic when Puntila explains to Matti the predicament which arises for him when he changes from an inebriated to a sober state. While drunk he is in possession of all his faculties, but these become impaired when he is sober. "Ich bin im vollen Besitz meiner Geisteskräfte, ich bin Herr meiner Sinne. Dann kommt der Anfall [sobriety]. Es beginnt damit, dass mit meinen Augen irgend etwas nicht mehr stimmt. Anstatt zwei Gabeln (er hebt eine Gabel hoch) sehe ich nur noch eine." And Matti's reply to this is: "Da sind Sie also halbblind?" (p. 11). ("I'm in full possession of all my mental faculties, I'm master of my senses. Then I get an attack [sobriety]. It starts with my eyes somehow or other not working right anymore. Instead of two forks [he lifts one fork] I only see one."—"Then you're actually half blind?") Granted that according to the Marxist view Puntila, halfblind, is

---

[5] *Versuche 22–24* (Berlin: Suhrkamp Verlag, 1950).

hardly worthy of human company, still he is a man. Even he should be capable of learning, of receiving instruction. Why should a special insight be given him only when he is full of wine. Is he a damned soul for whom there can be no possibility of redemption? Granted that his two different personalities are a handy device for communist dialectics, it would seem that this juggling of a fully perceptive drunken state and a half-blind sober state really weakens the argument. When Matti and the drunken Puntila climb a "Hatelmaberg" constructed of smashed furniture on top a billiard table inside Puntila's library (p. 84 ff.) in order to get a wide view of their beloved Finland, does this *gestus* mean that Puntila, like Moses, is looking on the promised land which he will never be allowed to enter? Or does the drunkenness of Puntila imply that conversion, the transformation of man, is no more profound or permanent than the happy, affable state of mind produced by imbibing alcohol? One can of course reconcile this with Marxist teaching: First change the outer conditions; the inner changes will then be easily accomplished. But this would repudiate to some extent the teaching of such a drama as "Die Mutter" in which the heroine, Pelagea Wlassowa, does learn and is converted. To be sure the convert here is a proletarian. This differentiation between Pelagea Wlassowa and Puntila and the consequent success or failure of conversion adds a tone of Old Testament self-righteousness and inexorable severity to the class-struggle. However, by using intoxication in *Herr Puntila und sein Knecht* in order to let this character speak truth in the manner of an inspired visionary Brecht leaves himself open to the wrong interpretation of his play. He was fully aware of this danger as becomes evident from his notes about the première performance in Zürich when he states: "Der Darsteller des Puntila muss sich hüten, in den Trunkenheitsszenen das Publikum durch Vitalität oder Charme so mitzureissen, dass ihm nicht mehr die Freiheit bleibt, ihn zu kritisieren."[6] ("The actor

[6] *Notizen 10,* p. 111.

portraying Puntila must take care in the drunken scenes not to enrapture the audience by his vitality or charm to such a degree that they are not free anymore to criticize him [the character].") But there is a third type of *gestus* which is in many ways the most puzzling and at the same time most revealing. This type of *gestus* is seen best in the drama *Mutter Courage und ihre Kinder*.[7] The main carrier of this mode of expression in the play is, of course, Kattrin, Mother Courage's mute daughter. Brecht himself has explained the function of this character, but I would like to discuss it purely from the evidence of the drama itself. Kattrin, since she is incapable of speech, can communicate only by gestures. She is the third of Mother Courage's children, the sister of Eilif, the bold son, and Schweizerkas, the honest son. She is referred to by the author himself in the title to scene 11 as "der Stein." It has a curious impact when in the scene in which Kattrin saves the town of Halle from destruction by Imperial troops—we read in the scene caption: "Der Stein beginnt zu reden." Kattrin, the stone, of course still speaks only in gestures. From the roof of a farmhouse outside the town she beats the drum which awakens the sleeping town to its danger and thereby makes it possible for them to repulse the enemy attack. Kattrin is killed by the enemy soldiers who are trying to silence her. When we examine the character of Kattrin more closely all through the play we find that she, who is the very personification of non-verbal expression of *gestus,* communicates most clearly when Mother Courage, the war profiteer, usually so voluble and active, is forced into inactivity, silence, or is not present at all. Kattrin's communication is always clear and to the point, even when she arranges with spiteful suggestiveness her Mother's apron and the trousers of the man who is trying to persuade Mother Courage to set up housekeeping with him and without Kattrin.

[7] *Versuche 20–21* (Berlin: Suhrkamp Verlag, 1957).

Kattrin is the most significant figure of Mother Courage's three children. She loses her life because of the war, as do her brothers, but where the oldest brother's death is a consequence of his robbing and killing in order to feed the troops, and the second brother's death is a consequence of his trying to save the regimental cash box, she dies saving the men, women and children of Halle. It is the pure humanity of her final act which sets her above her brothers. Is it not curious, then, that Brecht has not allowed this one genuinely good and kind person, who seems to have all the straight-forward, elemental virtues of womanhood, to communicate in words?

This non-verbal expression of Kattrin represents a language which comes straight from the heart, is never ambiguous, and is always imbued with a higher morality than that of any of the other characters in the play. I would like to call this "truthful" *gestus*. I realize that my choice of terms here would not meet with Brecht's approval; however, it seems to me that it is symbolic that when Brecht himself wishes to express pure, human emotion or a pure, unambivalent human reaction he takes recourse not to language but to *gestus*. An explanation of this may be found in *Fünf Schwierigkeiten beim Schreiben der Wahrheit*[8] ("Five difficulties in writing the truth"). In these five essays, entitled "Der Mut, die Wahrheit zu schreiben" (The courage to write the truth), "Die Klugheit, die Wahrheit zu erkennen" (The intelligence to recognize the truth), "Die Kunst, die Wahrheit handhabbar zu machen als eine Waffe" (The art to make the truth operative as a weapon), "Das Urteil, jene auszuwählen, in deren Händen die Wahrheit wirksam wird" (The judgment to choose those in whose hands the truth becomes effective), and "Die List, die Wahrheit unter vielen zu verbreiten" (The trick of spreading the truth among many), it becomes quite clear first of all, that the truth he speaks about is Marxist truth. Secondly, the

[8] *Versuche 20–21.*

manner in which this truth is to be written is determined by the fact that language, as a part of the capitalistic system, is basically treacherous. Since language is a tool of communication originally developed and used in a non-Marxist society, it incorporates in it all the faults of the society itself, and being a tool of the capitalistic rulers, it of necessity embodies deception and lies. To speak the truth, Brecht says, it is therefore necessary to turn these capitalistic lies into Marxist truth. Thus the capitalistic word *Volk* (people) becomes in the Marxist language *Bevölkerung* (population), *Boden* (soil) becomes *Landbesitz* (landed property), *Attentat* (assassination) becomes *Hinrichtung* (execution).[9] But does an inverted lie become a truth? All we actually have is a compounded lie. A biased view changed into another bias does not produce truth.

It seems to me, therefore, that "truthful" *gestus* symbolizes a deep distrust on Brecht's part of the spoken or written word, a distrust which is not based on the inherent ambiguity of language itself which grows out of the imperfection of human nature. This distrust of the word has worried many authors and seems to be the particular problem of the modern poet and writer.

[9] This use of language fits right in with Brecht's whole idea concerning the image of the world as represented by the artist. Here also inexactitude and even absurdities do not bother Brecht, as paragraph 9 of the "Kleines Organon für das Theater" shows: "Und man muss sich vor Augen halten, dass das Vernügen an den Abbildungen so verschiedener Art kaum jomals von dem Grad der Aehlichkeit des Abbilds mit dem Abgebildeten abhing. Unkorrektheit, selbst starke Unwahrscheinlichkeit störte wenig oder gar nicht, sofern nur die Unkorrektheit eine gewisse Konsistenz hatte und die Unwahrscheinlichkeit von derselben Art blieb" (*Versuche 27–32* [Berlin: Suhrkamp Verlag, 1958], p. 112). ("And one must remember that the pleasure in representations of such varied kinds hardly ever depended on the degree of similarity between the image and that which it represented. Incorrectness, even considerable improbability, was hardly if at all disturbing, so long as the incorrectness had a certain consistency, and the improbability remained of the same kind.")

The distrust which Brecht has—it seems to me—arises from the very use to which he puts language. He must have been aware that his own dialectic acrobatics make the spoken word a most untrustworthy vehicle for truth. How else, then, can it be, that he seems to feel that simple human truth can be conveyed only through *gestus?*

ANIMAL IMAGERY IN KATHERINE ANNE PORTER'S FICTION

Sister M. Joselyn, O.S.B.
College of St. Scholastica

In an eminently just and perceptive estimate, Edmund Wilson wrote in 1944 that Katherine Anne Porter's style is "of a purity and precision almost unique in contemporary literature," but went on to say that "her writing itself makes a surface so smooth that the critic has little opportunity to point out peculiarities of color or weave."[1] Earlier, in 1939, Glenway Wescott had taken very much the same view when he concluded that Katherine Anne Porter's "is rather a bare art. It is not corporeal or sensual: the colors in it are primary: the odors evocative only in the general way, inoffensive to the average nostril: the shapes of things not geometrical or richly similitudinous: the faces not fussed over."[2] And Joseph Warren Beach, less positive in his assertion, found (1950) that "There is a perhaps deceptive quietness in her tone."[3]

If these critics mean merely to emphasize that Miss Porter's language never calls attention to itself one can surely concur, but if they mean that it is an anonymous style, they need to re-examine the question. There is at least one distinguishing mark in Miss Porter's most distinguished fiction, and that is a consistent use of imagery relating human beings to animals and

---

[1] "Katherine Ann Porter," *New Yorker*, XX (1944), 72–75. Reprinted in Edmund Wilson's *Classics and Commercials* (New York: Farrar, Straus, 1950), p. 219.

[2] "Praise," *Southern Review*, V (1939), 168.

[3] "Self-Consciousness and Its Antidotes," *Virginia Quarterly Review*, XXI (1945), 292.

animal life. Miss Porter, however, does not merely employ the same "dead" or conventional animal imagery that we all do—she does write of men "dying like flies," of children who "ran wild" or might grow up "hog wild," of a woman "with a back like a mule," of a man who "fought like a wildcat" and was "killed like a mad dog"—but she creates a surprising profusion of freshly invented animal images, primarily metaphors and similes but also including some symbols, and uses them with the control and precision one expects in a craftsman of her talents. The present examination of animal imagery is based on six representative fictions by Miss Porter: *Flowering Judas* (from the volume of that title published in 1930), *Pale Horse, Pale Rider* (from the volume of that title published in 1939), *The Leaning Tower* (from the volume of that title published in 1944), "The Circus" (in *The Leaning Tower*), "The Downward Path to Wisdom" (in *The Leaning Tower*), and *Ship of Fools* (1962).[4] All of these stories contain significant animal imagery fulfilling at least four basic functions: (1) it serves as a major device of characterization, (2) it assists in defining and limiting the terms of conflict, (3) it establishes tone, and (4) it concretizes and dramatizes value judgments.[5]

[4] References in this study are to the following editions and pages: *Flowering Judas,* from *Flowering Judas and Other Stories* (New York: Modern Library, 1940), pp. 139–160; *The Leaning Tower,* pp. 149–246, "The Circus," pp. 21–32, "The Downward Path to Wisdom," pp. 81–114, from *The Leaning Tower and Other Stories* (New York: Harcourt, Brace, 1944); *Pale Horse, Pale Rider,* from the volume of that title (New York: Modern Library, 1949), pp. 179–264; and *Ship of Fools* (Boston: Atlantic-Little, Brown, 1962).

[5] Others who have briefly noted Miss Porter's use of animal imagery are James W. Johnson, who suggests that "weak or vicious people are figuratively animalistic: they are 'penguins' or they have 'rabbit teeth' or 'skunk heads'" ("Another Look at Katherine Anne Porter," *Virginia Quarterly Review,* XXXVI [1960], 610), and Charles Kaplan, who refers to the animal imagery in "The Circus" ("True Witness: Katherine Anne Porter," *Colorado Quarterly,* VII [1959], 323).

As her readers know, Miss Porter's major device for rendering character is interior conversation shown as thought, reverie, or dream, and she employs dialogue and physical action in the normal manner. But it should not be overlooked that a more purely stylistic device such as animal imagery also has an important place in revealing consciousness and consciences. These animal images are deployed in various ways: spaced throughout the longer fictions, where they reinforce other character-creating devices, employed with a climactic effect to characterize groups of people, rapidly sketched in in the form of metaphors that distinguish particular members of these groups, or as what might be called iterative series, when they lead to caricaturization if the theme is thin or the conception of character stale.

The figure of Braggioni in *Flowering Judas* is an example of a marvellously rounded creation devised partly through explicit statement, an elaborate net of contrasts, and a complex religious and anti-religious symbolism. But none of these means is more effective in conveying a sense of the nature of Braggioni than five or six animal figures. In the first sentence we see through the eyes of Laura the figure of Braggioni who "sits heaped upon the edge of a straight-backed chair much too small for him, and sings to Laura in a furry, mournful voice." He is "snarling a tune under his breath" (p. 139). Soon the revolutionary is described as he "scratches the guitar familiarly as though it were a pet animal, and sings passionately off key, taking the high notes in a prolonged painful squeal" (p. 140), and we begin to perceive the nature of the threat which surrounds Laura, a threat which, as it happens, she both courts and resists. We learn to feel more about the danger when we are told that as Braggioni "stretches his eyelids at Laura she notes again that his eyes are the true tawny yellow cat's eyes" (p. 148). Later these "ill-humored cat's eyes" are said to "waver in a separate glance for the two points of light marking the opposite ends of a smoothly drawn path between the swollen curves of her breasts" (p. 152).

When Braggioni sighs, "his leather belt creaks like a saddle girth" (p. 144). A kind of final evaluation of Braggioni—violent, corrupt, brutal, narcissistic, sensual, voracious—is reached when, not far from the end of the story, Laura ruminates that "He will live to see himself kicked out from his feeding trough by other hungry world saviors" (pp. 152–153). It may be remarked in passing, though, that the frigid, locked-in, "angelic" Laura no more achieves her humanity than does the beast-like Braggioni; the story's action is essentially a kind of trance-like motion of the satyr around the virgin in which the outcome is pre-determined by Laura's deep will to be devoured and Braggioni's instinctive certainty of that will.

Braggioni is illustrative of Miss Porter's employment of animal figures as a device for psychologically placing a single protagonist, but she is also extremely skilled in the use of animal images to describe groups or masses of people. Her portrayal of *entre guerre* Germans in *The Leaning Tower* and *Ship of Fools* is a case in point. Here her purpose is not so much the differentiation of individuals as it is the recreation of certain mass attitudes or psychoses. The famous scene in *The Leaning Tower* (pp. 159–160) when Charles Upton observes a group of Berliners staring fascinatedly at a holiday shopwindow shows the device at its most effective:

He had watched a group of middle-aged men and women who were gathered in silence before two adjoining windows, gazing silently at displays of toy pigs and sugar pigs. These persons were all strangely of a kind, and strangely the most prevalent type. The streets were full of them—enormous waddling women with short legs and ill-humored faces, and round-headed men with great rolls of fat across the backs of their necks, who seemed to support their swollen bellies with an effort that drew their shoulders forward. Nearly all of them were leading their slender, overbred, short-legged dogs in pairs on fancy leashes. The dogs wore their winter clothes: wool sweaters, fur ruffs, and fleece-lined rubber boots. The creatures whined and complained and shivered, and their owners lifted them up tenderly to show them the pigs.

In one window there were sausages, hams, bacon, small pink chops; all pig, real pig, fresh, smoked, salted, baked, roasted, pickled, spiced, and jellied. In the other were dainty artificial pigs, almond paste pigs, pink sugar chops, chocolate sausages, tiny hams and bacons of melting cream streaked and colored to the very life. Among the tinsel and lace paper, at the back were still other kinds of pigs: plush pigs, black velvet pigs, spotted cotton pigs, metal and wooden mechanical pigs, all with frolicsome curled tails and appealing infant faces.

With their nervous dogs wailing in their arms, the people, shameless mounds of fat, stood in a trance of pig worship, gazing with eyes damp with admiration and appetite. They resembled the most unkind caricatures of themselves, but they were the very kind of people that Holbein and Durer and Ura Graf had drawn, too: not vaguely, but positively like, their late-medieval faces full of hallucinated malice and a kind of sluggish but intense cruelty that worked its way up from their depths slowly through the layers of helpless gluttonous fat.

The scene of course both dramatizes the moral condition of pre-World War II Berlin and furthers the plot of the story, which is basically an account of the initiation of Charles Upton, the naive American art student. Witnessing the Berliners before the pig-display pushes Charles one step further along the reluctant path of his discoveries.

In *Ship of Fools,* Miss Porter's strategy often resembles that in *The Leaning Tower* as she depicts the journey of a group of passengers, predominantly German, leaving Vera Cruz for Bremerhaven and the fatherland. Since the story is novel-length, we find the Germans making up this shipboard group depicted in more detail than most of the Germans in *The Leaning Tower,* but their cruelty, their smugness and chauvinism, their greed and sentimentality, their imperviousness to the most elementary truths of human relationships, are again portrayed in animal terms. On shipboard, the American Mrs. Treadwell notices that "too often the very nicest Germans wolfed their food" (p. 139), while the guests at the Captain's table are shown as falling upon "their splendid full-bodied German food with hot appetites," pausing occasionally "to wipe their teeming mouths, nodding at each other in silence" (p. 40). Wilhelm Freytag, whose duty it is to return to his native land to rescue his Jewish wife, nevertheless sees himself as "altogether German," with the whole world "for him merely a hunting ground, a foraging place" (p. 134). For the deported sugar workers whom the Captain has crushed into the steerage like "so many head of cattle" (p. 172), Freytag confesses he feels "an instinctive contempt and distrust," for these and all the "swarming poor spawned like maggots in filth, befouling the air around them." "What kind of creature," he asks himself, "would endure this, except a lower order of animal?" (p. 134). Captain Thiele simply feels it "beneath his dignity . . . to admit any human meaning or importance in the doings of the rabble in the steerage" (p. 173).

Once Miss Porter has concretely established the nature and extent of the German malaise, she turns her attention to particular persons within the group, now utilizing images drawn from animal life to depict specific individuals. Thus Rosa, the landlady in *The Leaning Tower,* scurries, swarms, flutes, and whimpers; Van Bussen the suicidal mathematics student looks at a cabaret girl "with the calculating ferocity of a tomcat" (p. 241) and eats "offal" but asserts in a drunken fit of confidence that "We are not by any means all the pig type" (p. 224); Hans the self-scarred Heidelberg duelist has outer lids that give him "the look of a young, intelligent fox" (p. 189), watches his filling brandy glass "as if he would spring upon it" (p. 190) and calls the

French "a race of monkeys" (p. 227); the prostitutes are bird-like in their feathered hats; the landlord's "pale little eyes behind their puffy lids were piggish with malice" (p. 170) and his jibing laughter makes him and his wife seem to Charles "like a pair of hyenas" (p. 172). On the "Ship of Fools" the grotesque Lizzie Spokenkieker is shown "screaming like a peahen in German at her companion, a little dumpling of a man, pink and pig-snouted" (p. 12); while Johann the boy-nurse bears "the look of an outcast dog for longing and hopelessness" (p. 126), cursing his corpse-like uncle as "a beast of selfishness" (p. 74). Here also the sentimental widow Rittersdorf laments the loss of a deck-chair pillow made of "pure white goose down . . . sent to her from Germany all the way to Mexico as for a Christmas present from her dear dead husband's dear mother" (p. 82) and bares her teeth at Herr Rieber as she inwardly pronounces him "pig-dog" (p. 287). Here also is the obese Frau Hutten, whose surrogate baby is an English bulldog, and who draws from her pompous professor husband the expression of "a strong innocent man gazing into a pit of cobras" (p. 295).

Obviously, the effect of the animal imagery in passages like these is to create something close to caricature, appropriate as that may be for writing conducted in a satirical vein. It is worthy of note, however, that the effect of caricature through animal imagery is occasionally carried over into narratives where it is inappropriate, such as "The Downward Path to Wisdom," where the relatively ineffective handling of theme and characterization betrays itself in a monotony of similes comparing the child Stephen to a lamb. But when, as in "The Circus," the animal imagery at once depicts character and provides a structural framework, we have a very fine story indeed. It is animal figures used by Dicey the Negro nurse early in this story which set the tone and suggest the major conflicts. In the first paragraph we are shown the tent packed with people who appear to Dicey " 'lak flies on a dog's ear' " (p. 21). Soon afterwards, Dicey's warning to

Miranda about the circus boys playing beneath the plank seats is also couched in animal terms: "You just mind y'o own business. . . . Plenty o' monkeys right here in the show widout you studyin dat kind" (pp. 22–23). Built upon a series of experiences which constitute Miranda's introduction into the meaning of adult life, the story begins with the child's discovery of the peeping circus boys

> squatted in little heaps, staring up quietly. She looked squarely into the eyes of one, who returned her a look so peculiar she gazed and gazed, trying to understand it. It was a bold grinning stare without any kind of friendliness in it. [p. 22]

Miranda's second revelation coincides with the appearance of the clown:

> A creature in a blousy white overall with ruffles at the neck and ankles, with bone-white skull and chalk-white face, with tufted eyebrows far apart in the middle of his forehead, the lids in a black sharp angle, a long scarlet mouth stretching back into sunken cheeks, turned up at the corners in a perpetual bitter grimace of pain, astonishment, not smiling, pranced along a wire stretched down the center of the ring. . . . High above their heads the inhuman figure pranced . . . . He paused, slipped, the flapping white leg waved in space; he staggered, wobbled, slipped sidewise, plunged, and caught the wire with frantic knee, hanging there upside down, the other leg waving like a feeler above his head . . . . [pp. 23–24]

The third shock of revelation comes when Miranda experiences what is happening to the human audience while the clown performs, for she sees with astonishment that the crowd "roared with savage delight," and shrieked with "dreadful laughter like devils in delicious torment" (p. 24).[6] Meanwhile, the clown has

[6] The human-to-beast-to-devil metamorphosis will also be repeated in Miranda's encounter with the dwarf. It is found also in the career of Ric and Rac in *Ship of Fools,* and in various other places.

become an almost obsessional half-human, half-animal figure: "The man on the wire, hanging by his foot, turned his head like a seal from side to side and blew sneering kisses from his cruel mouth. Then Miranda covered her eyes and screamed. . . ." (p. 24).

The fourth moment of confrontation comes when Miranda and Dicey, making their way out of the tent, meet a dwarf described in demon-like images as "wearing a little woolly beard, a pointed cap, tight red breeches, long shoes with turned-up toes." At first the dwarf "leaned forward and peered" at Miranda "with kind, not-human golden eyes, like a near-sighted dog," but then it "made a horrid grimace at her, imitating her own face." The nurse drew her away, but "not before Miranda had seen in his face . . . a look of haughty, remote displeasure, a true grown-up look. . . . It chilled her with a new kind of fear: she had not believed he was really human" (pp. 24–25). At home, later, the other children's memories consist of "wonderful little ponies with plumes and bells on their bridles, ridden by darling little monkeys in velvet jackets and peaked hats . . . trained white goats that danced . . . a baby elephant that crossed his front feet and leaned against his cage and opened his mouth to be fed, *such* a baby! . . . more clowns, funnier than the first one even," ladies who hung gracefully by their toes "like flying birds!" (p. 26), but for Miranda, these childish visions will not do. "She tried, as if she were really remembering them, to think of the beautiful wild beings in white satin and spangles and red sashes who danced and frolicked on the trapezes; of the sweet furry little ponies and the lovely pet monkeys in their comical clothes" (p. 27). Yet when she fell asleep, "her invented memories gave way before her real ones, the bitter terrified face of the man in blousy white falling to his death . . . and the terrible grimace of the unsmiling dwarf" (pp. 27-28). Miss Porter thus successfully dramatizes Miranda's induction into the universe of moral and metaphysical evil, utilizing animal imagery as an important structural and linguistic element in this portrayal.

In *Pale Horse, Pale Rider* where theme is again partly developed through animal imagery we again witness a story structured as the nightmarish oscillation of a sensitive protagonist between the animal and human worlds while the experience of evil is forced upon her. This short novel employs a good deal of sharply conceived minor animal imagery as in Miranda's thoughts about the predatory Liberty Bond salesman, in her view of the barracks that "swarmed and worked with an aimless life of scurrying, dun-colored insects" (p. 193), where she may meet a "jolly hungry puppy glad of a bite to eat and a little chatter" (p. 193). The eyes of Bill the city editor she sees as "soft and lambent but wild, like a stag's" (p. 211), while Chuck the sports editor explains of his army rejection, "I've offered my meat to the crows and they won't have it" (p. 216).

But animal figures are used more meaningfully in the story's superb controlling symbol, the horse of death, and in the main thematic development, Miranda's efforts to transcend the physical illness which stands for the entire moral and spiritual struggle that constitutes human existence. Even before her illness Miranda observes of a crowd of playgoers, "we dare not say a word to each other of our desperation, we are speechless animals letting ourselves be destroyed. . . ." (pp. 218–219).

In the hospital "She struggled to cry out, saying, Let me go, let me go; but heard only incoherent sounds of animal suffering" (p. 255), while in the central action of the story, the delirious dream of death which enacts the girl's deepest desire—to die and become a part of the luring jungle—Miranda sees a tall sailing ship, and behind it

a jungle, and even as it appeared before her, she knew it was all she had ever read or had been told or felt or thought about jungles; a writhing terribly alive and secret place of death, creeping with tangles of spotted serpents, rainbow-colored birds with malign eyes, leopards with humanly wise faces and extravagantly crested lions; screaming long-armed monkeys tumbling among broad fleshy leaves that glowed with sulphur-colored light and exuded the ichor of death, and rotting trunks of unfamiliar trees sprawled in crawling slime. Without surprise . . . she saw herself run swiftly down this gangplank. . . . The air trembled with the shattering scream and the hoarse bellow of voices all crying together . . . . [pp. 231–232]

Miranda does not die but, having attained the knowledge of good and evil, finds in life "No more war, no more plague, only . . . noiseless houses with the shades drawn, empty streets, the dead cold light of tomorrow" (p. 264). In this world, there is no place, either, for the now-dead Adam who had been "Pure . . . all the way through, flawless, complete, as the sacrificial lamb must be" (p. 224), and he too had been destroyed.

Other stories, like *The Leaning Tower,* which employ animal imagery as a leading structural device, are created out of tension between the known "human" world and the gradually revealed "beast" world which surrounds and threatens it. *Ship of Fools,* for instance, is in part patterned from the contrast between the world of the steerage ("there rose from the steerage a long hoarse blood-curdling howl like a pack of coyotes" as "the shapeless dark mass huddled and heaped, leaning far out and over, working madly within itself as if the people were all entangled and could not break apart" [p. 313]), and the world of the upper decks peopled by the inhuman Germans. The Germans' moral identity is defined through their reactions to the life of the steerage as Miss Porter demonstrates that the passengers of the upper decks have surrendered their humanity precisely in destroying that of others. Animal imagery is also important in the episodes narrating the depredations of the demonic Spanish twins Ric and Rac among the "beastly" passengers. Denny, an American, notes that after one of their malignant tricks the twins "scurried past with wide eyes and open mouth, tongues strained out of the corners, crazy as ever" (p. 313). Prying upon the amorous play of Herr

Reiber and Lizzi Spokenkieker, they approached discreetly holding each other back, "as little foxes ... for fear the other would get the first glimpse, exchanging shrewd glances, the whites of their eyes gleaming, their pointed red tongues running around their open mouths" (p. 194). To most of the passengers, the twins are "outside the human race" (p. 330), while the more balanced Dr. Schumann describes them as "little monsters," and calls them "Devil-possessed" (p. 198).

Structurally, then, the animal imagery in Miss Porter's stories implicitly creates the non-human and partially human levels through which her protagonists struggle to grasp meaning and to fulfill themselves. As a device for establishing tone, moreover, the animal imagery both arouses and focuses attention, for as Elder Olson has pointed out, images "by *themselves* can 1) force the mind to supplement, rearrange, and augment, 2) produce other images, 3) cause inferences, 4) induce emotions and trains of emotion."[7] Animal images frequently occur near the beginnings of the stories, and almost always at climactic moments; thus Miss Porter induces emotions and trains of emotion. Foreboding, fear, dread, revulsion, something atavistic and defensive is aroused deep within the reader and is strengthened as the action unfolds until we experience the story with a degree of excitement and involvement unusual for the types of themes and plots this author handles. Note, for example, the intensity of feeling both described and re-created in the reader in the following passages:

> It was then that the beggar woman, fiercely as a pouncing hawk, had darted out her long hard claws, seized a fold of flesh near the shoulder and wrung it, wrung it bitterly, her nails biting into the skin ... Well, it had been like a bad dream. [*Ship of Fools*, p. 14]

[7] "The Poetry of Wallace Stevens," *College English*, XVI (April, 1955), 402.

... she stood transfixed, lips parted, unable to breathe a syllable, with his black eyes like a snake's gleaming wickedly only a few inches from hers, and had felt herself taken without her consent and spirited away....

[*Ship of Fools*, p. 269]

She began, "They are all over the shops, everywhere, like a pack of invading rats. I have watched them, and I know they are stealing right and left." [*Ship of Fools*, p. 382]

Charles, at the foot of the bed, had a curious scene flash through his mind: Herr Bussen, the object of charity, fleeing like a stag across the snowy waste, with Hans and Tadeusz and Rose and he, Charles, after him in full cry, bringing him down, by the throat if necessary, to give him aid and comfort. Charles heard the deep mournful voices of his father's liver-spotted hounds.

[*The Leaning Tower*, p. 214]

By selecting powerful images from a particularly evocative field of reference, Miss Porter at once arouses certain kinds of emotions and also controls and directs the reader's feelings with something like the precision and subtlety of the poet.

To point to Miss Porter's use of animal imagery to describe character and to define the structural elements of her stories is to state implicitly that she also employs this imagery in a fourth function, the rendering of value judgments. From a purely statistical point of view, it is clear that the majority of figures in the six stories under consideration are composed with a "vehicle" drawn from wild animal life. Katherine Anne Porter is of course not interested in animals for their own sake, but turns to them only as referents by which she can dramatize and evaluate human types and human actions, or, as Wallace Fowlie says (of a very different kind of user of animal imagery, Marianne Moore), "represent simultaneously in a single name both a spiritual world and a human being."[8]

[8] *Sewanee Review*, LX (1952), 541.

Writing of Thomas Hardy's belief that "human nature is not grounded in common sense, that there is a deep place in it where the mind does not go, where the blind monsters sleep and wake, war among themselves and feed upon death," Miss Porter would seem to concur.[9] For her, the only human—or moral— world is created out of an incessant struggle with the animal forces around and within the individual. It is a perilous existence at best, for at any moment these forces may erupt, and even the most sensitive and courageous individuals are never really safe. They have no more than their integrity and strength of will to pit against the dark forces from below.

Thus the child Miranda of "The Circus" awkens to the discovery of dark, irrational forces which will be a permanent presence, and the Miranda of *Pale Horse, Pale Rider,* though an adult, has only encountered evil under more varied guises. Stephen in "The Downward Path to Wisdom" knows as he practices his incantation against existence—"I hate Papa, I hate Mama, I hate Grandma, I hate Uncle David, I hate Old Janet, I hate Marjory, I hate Papa. I hate Mama . . ." (p. 111)—that he will be devoured by his beastlike elders; for Charles Upton, there is only one conceivable end of the reign of "smiling foxes, famished wolves, slovenly housecats, mere tigers, hyenas, furies, harpies" of Berlin (*The Leaning Tower,* p. 162), and that is destruction. To some readers, indeed, Katherine Anne Porter's world is "a black and tragic one, filled with disaster, heartbreak, and soul-wrecking disillusionment."[10] But whether or not one finds this so, or accepts Miss Porter's total view of life, it must be conceded that, given her particular vision of human existence, she has chosen with great skill an appropriate field of imagery through which to dramatize her sense of the moral life. As George

[9] "On a Criticism of Thomas Hardy," 1940. Reprinted in Katherine Anne Porter's *The Days Before* (New York: Harcourt, Brace, 1952), p. 31.
[10] James W. Johnson, (see note 5, above), p. 169.

T. Wright has remarked, "Even the most detached reporter implies through his choice of subject and his choice of words an attitude toward what he reports, and in good writing this attitude will be consistent enough to be intelligible as a point of view."[11]

---

[11] George T. Wright, *The Poet in the Poem* (Berkeley: University of California Press, 1960), p. 27.

APPLICATIONS (II)

The Work Examined: Archetypes and Interpretations

CHASTITY, REGENERATION, AND WORLD ORDER IN
ALL'S WELL THAT ENDS WELL

Eric LaGuardia
University of Washington

In this paper I want to deal with *All's Well that Ends Well* in terms of what I believe to be its major poetic objective: to dramatize the regeneration of man and imitate the condition of *concordia mundi*. The play can be read as dramatic metaphor reconciling what Greville called nature's "diverse laws," and representing what Sidney would have called a golden rather than a brazen world. In its presentation of a progression from the unregenerate to the regenerate condition, the play reflects the Renaissance interest in the idea of the renewal of nature and the worldly perfection of man.

In terms of a major problem in the history of ideas, the conflict which the play sets out to resolve is nature vs. spirit. The action of the play and its dramatic conventions, of course, do not explicitly touch upon an issue of such magnitude. That is, the play is not philosophically sophisticated, but its figurative or symbolic range relates the action and theme to issues more inclusive than those literally represented in its courtly and romantic setting. More immediate to what actually happens in the play, and thus more pertinent to an analysis of the drama, is the conflict between passion and purity. On this level the play can be taken for what quite literally it is: a romantic drama of the conflicts of love. However, the problem of nature vs. spirit is not unrelated to the problem of passion vs. purity. The idea of purity in *All's Well,* manifested in the figure of Helena, is quite explicitly related to the divine world beyond nature with all those

119

connotations of virtue, eternal order, and perfection it had for the English Renaissance. And the idea of passion, manifested in one of its important forms in the figure of Parolles, is related to the lowest level of nature with its corruptions, imperfections, and vices.

The problem which the play sets out to resolve is a conflict which occurs wholly within the natural world. In other words, the objective of the drama is not to resolve the conflict *between* the natural world and the divine world, but rather to resolve the conflict *within* the natural world between that level of nature which most intimately touches the divine world above, and that level of nature which most intimately touches the demonic world below. In addition, that very interesting symbolic function of chastity made clear to us by Professor Woodhouse and others is, I think, at work in Shakespeare's play. Chastity in *All's Well*, embodied in the character of Helena, is a redemptive force which has as its content elements of both the divine and the natural world. Its effect on the world of the play is the ultimate resolution of the tension between passion and purity—in the ideal of chaste love. The special characteristics of this resolution will be made clear in the course of the following analysis. At this point I simply want to state the general conclusions to which I have come in studying this play. *All's Well* should be read more figuratively than, I believe, it has been in the past. It is a symbolic drama with the objective of reconciling the extremities of the laws of nature, represented in the play by the romantic problem of passion vs. purity. The reconciliation is made in terms of the concord of chaste love, which is, taken metaphorically, an image of *concordia mundi*.

In the following analysis I concentrate on two regenerative narrative actions in the play—initiation and purification; on the interaction of the divine and natural world through Helena and her chastity; and on the nature of the resolution toward which the play moves. At the conclusion of the paper I suggest a relationship between formal aspects of the play and the intellectual preoccupations of the age in which it was written. To give clarity to this relationship I have employed some of the ideas of Northrop Frye and Erich Auerbach, respectively, to identify relevant formal and intellectual characteristics of *All's Well*. The special equilibrium between the natural and the divine which the play ultimately asserts is (in Frye's terms) the balance maintained in the "romantic mode" between the totally mythic and a more plausible representation of reality. This same equilibrium is a reflection of what Auerbach would describe as the decline of figural mimesis in the direction of secular mimesis. Thus, the formal and historical concerns of Frye and Auerbach both confirm the particular structural and intellectual nature of Shakespeare's play.

All's Well that Ends Well begins in disorder and ends in order. At the start the old Count of Rousillon is dead (and presumably the great tradition of virtue and nobility with him), leaving Bertram, the new Count, without a father, and his mother without a husband. Helena's father, a physician who possessed remarkable healing powers, is also dead. The King of France is suffering from a fistula; and the Florentines are in need of French aid in their wars. From a more romantic standpoint, Helena is in love with Bertram, but is unable to find a way to circumvent or destroy the social as well the emotional barrier between them. And Bertram, heir to the Rousillon tradition, seems to promise very little beside his handsome figure for the fulfillment of his noble birthright. These circumstances with which the play begins define a society of immaturity and disorder in which Helena and Bertram have individual destinies to fulfill. The terms set up in this romantic comedy indicate that Helena must establish a rightful union with Bertram; and that Bertram must renounce his profligate ways and become fit to bear the name of Rousillon. In addition to problems of unrequited love and unfulfilled birthright, the King of France requires a cure for his fistula, symbolic

121

of the restoration of the whole diseased court of France. These are the objectives of the action of the play; they involve both personal growth to maturity, and a large scale social integration.

With this background in mind it is possible to distinguish two motifs in the play: the actions of initiation and purification. It is evident that both these patterns of action are regenerative in effect, but I distinguish between them because of the different emphases they represent in the play.

The restorative motif of initiation involves both Helena and Bertram. In both cases the content of the life of the character is transformed. The processes of initiation, however, are different. Helena embarks with great determination on her quest for the love of Bertram, while Bertram is until the very last unwilling to acknowledge the change that is taking place in his life. In spite of her obvious determination to become initiated into the world of love, Helena is not without mixed feelings concerning the steps necessary for such an initiation. She both desires and fears the transformation from maid to woman. She recognizes that the initiation into womanhood can be accomplished only by sub-mission to sensuality, but she is determined that the submission shall not qualify the ultimate value of her chastity.

This ambivalance toward sensuality and purity is introduced in the first scene of the play in which Parolles and Helena are engaged in a discussion of virginity. Consistent with her status as a young virgin, Helena asks, "Man is enemy to virginity; how may we barricado it against him?" Parolles is scornful of such timidity, and much like Comus he argues that "it is not politic in the commonwealth of nature to preserve virginity. Loss of virginity is rational increase, and there was never virgin got till virginity was first lost." To his assertion that virginity violates the "rule of nature" Helena replies with the question: "How might one do, sir, to lose it to her own liking?" We can trace Helena's shift in attitude in this scene from an indignant, although playful, refusal even to consider the loss of virginity, to a cautious, and still playful, inquiry as to how she might lose it but still preserve her chasteness. In addition, the demonic function of Parolles is very pointed in this scene. He is a representative of the "naturalistic" or libertine point of view. His "rule of nature" is analogous to Comus' "covenant of nature," through which he invokes a false law of nature that does not take into account those demands of purity which align man and his world with the upper world of virtue and order. The entire scene expresses the conflict between those diverse laws of nature which troubled Greville. The conflict is made dramatic in terms of Helena's desire for, but fear of, an initiation into the world of passion or sensuality.

Helena, at the point of selecting Bertram for her husband as a reward for curing the King of France of his fistula, comes more fully to realize the significance of the decision facing her, as well as its difficulty.

> The blushes in my cheeks thus whisper me,
> "We blush that thou shold'st choose; but, be refused,
> Let the white death sit on thy cheek forever,
> We'll ne'er come there again."
>
> Now, Dian, from thy altar do I fly,
> And to imperial Love, that god most high,
> Do my sighs stream.   [II.iii.75–78, 81–83]

The decision facing her is, in short, a matter of life or death. It brings shame to a young virgin to choose love, but it brings a figurative death for a maid not to choose to be a woman. Helena's initiation is a matter of flying from the altar of Diana to the altar of Eros. Earlier in the play she reveals that she is aware of this transformation:

>   ... if yourself,
> Whose aged honour cites a virtuous youth,
> Did ever in so true a flame of liking

> Wish chastely and love dearly, that your Dian
> Was both herself and Love, O, then give pity
> To her, whose state is such that cannot choose . . .
> [I.III.215–20]

The single identity of Diana and Eros, indicated in this speech to the Countess, reveals Helena's objective in the play. The choice between love and perpetual virginity is presented to her in terms of life or death.

Virginity in this play is a condition which represents nature unfulfilled. The sensuality opposed to virginity may take two forms. It may be a "naturalizing" sensuality in Parolles' sense of the word, in which case nature is corrupted rather than fulfilled. Or it may be a sensuality tempered by chastity, in which case nature is pulled upward to a regenerate condition. This is the condition Helena looks forward to. It includes both the thorn of passion and the rose of innocence (as the Countess observes at one point in the play): Diana and Eros become a single force, fulfilling nature.

With the aid of the divine forces within her because of her chastity (which identifies her as an earthly counterpart of a heavenly virtue), Helena avoids the corrupt influence of Parolles and completes her initiation from maid to woman. The final stage of this journey into full feminine consciousness is completed with the help of the Florentine maid Diana, an earthly counterpart of the goddess of chastity. Through the substitution of herself for Diana, Helena proceeds from a virtual union with Bertram to a true union. Thus, through the character of the Florentine maid Helena's wish that the goddess Diana should be "both herself and Love" is eminently fulfilled.

The initiation of Bertram bears a close resemblance to that of Helena, for he also moves from youth to maturity and to the fulfillment of true love. His youthful condition, however, is one of ignorance and irresponsibility. We are informed at the start of the play that Bertram is heir to the noble birthright of

Rousillon, symbolized by the ring given him by his father, and which it is "the greatest obloquy i' th' world" to lose. "You must hold the credit of your father," he is told by Lafeu; but his activities through most of the play indicate he is unable to follow this advice. Parolles tempts Bertram to break the king's commandment which has kept him home, away from the Florentine wars. In this temptation we can recognize again the demonic function of Parolles in the play. Angered by his forced marriage to Helena, Bertram and Parolles leave for Florence.

The main stages of Bertram's initiation into a regenerate life of maturity and virtue are: the secret consummation of his marriage to Helena, and his rejection of Parolles—experiences which occur in direct sequence in the play. The importance of Bertram's unwitting union with Helena is underlined by the double stipulation which, ironically, he himself imposes on his wife:

When thou canst get the ring upon my finger which never shall come off, and show me a child begotten of thy body that I am father to, then call me husband. . . .
[III.ii.59–62]

The fulfillment of the second part of this sentence, accepted by Bertram at the end of the play, obviously constitutes the real marriage of the two figures, although Bertram at the time does not realize it. The removal of Bertram's ring which stands for the nobility of the Rousillon line, is a symbolic act which temporarily deprives him of the image of a nobility he does not yet deserve, and will not deserve until he comes to recognize the goodness of Helena and his love for her. In the final scene of the play, as he accepts Helena and their bond of chaste love, Bertram emerges from his folly and is fully initiated into a regenerate life of mature virtue.

While the motif of initiation serves to dramatize the experience of individuals, the motif of purification in the play dramatizes both individual and civil experiences. Helena is, again, the

125

most important figure. Her redemptive powers are stressed, and are clearly linked to her purity. Not only does the power of her purity allow her ultimately to experience the reality of chaste physical love, but it also serves to redeem the world of the play from its fallen condition. Her eminent qualifications as a redeemer are revealed to us in a variety of ways. The first hint of her unusual qualities comes in the form of a striking compliment paid to her father by the Countess. He was a man, she remarks, "whose skill was almost as great as his honesty; had it stretch'd so far, would have made nature immortal." We learn that she has inherited much of this virtue, and that her own personality contributes a power of goodness. The first real evidence of Helena's healing powers is her cure of the King of France. After a number of unsuccessful attempts by various doctors to heal his fistula, the king agrees to give Helena an opportunity. She asks him to trust in the help of heaven through her, and not merely in human skill; he begins to feel the miraculous power of the young virgin:

> Methinks in thee some blessed spirit doth speak
> His powerful sound within an organ weak...
>
> [II.i.178–9]

Helena's first act of purification, the healing of the sick king, has effects beyond that of simple medical health for one man. Earlier in the play the reader is led to believe that the whole court has its share of corruptions, symbolic of which is the sickness of the king himself. Thus, in curing the King of France Helena has performed a symbolic act indicative of the purification of the entire courtly world.

Somewhat ironically, Parolles and Lafeu give us the most explicit testimony to the redemptive powers of Helena. Lafeu recognizes that in her there is "a showing of heavenly effect in an earthly actor." Their discussion continues in this way:

126

Par. Nay, 'tis strange, 'tis very strange, that is the brief
    and the tedious of it; and he's of a most facinerous
    spirit that will not acknowledge it to be the—
Laf. Very hand of Heaven.
Par. Ay, so I say.
Laf. In a most weak—
Par. And debile minister, great power, great transcend-
    ence; which should, indeed, give us further use to be
    made than alone the recovery of the King, as to be—
Laf. Generally thankful.

[II.iii.33–43]

This brief, comic, antiphonal exchange has, I think, an important
metaphorical function in the play. It attests to Helena's connection with the divine world, it extends the significance of her act
of healing beyond the mere recovery of the king, and the last
phrase, "generally thankful," is expressive of the whole regenerative theme of the play—the reintegration of the society, the return
of purity and order reflected in the king's speech on the ideal
concept of nobility, the resolution of Helena's love conflict, the
restoration of the prodigal Bertram, and the ultimate purgation
of the demonic influence of Parolles.

The most important part of Bertram's purification is the
ritualized consummation of his marriage to Helena which fulfills the conditions of a true marriage set down in his letter to
her. The fulfillment of those conditions which were made to
seem impossible, and the device of substituting Helena for Diana
are figurative ways of indicating that Bertram's proper destiny
is not only to fulfill his birthright, but also to be joined to
Helena by the bond of true love. In fact, the first is contingent
upon the second. He does not fully assume his role as the new
Count of Rousillon until he is able to acknowledge Helena as
his true wife.

Parolles is the final barrier between Bertram and his redemption; but the removal of the influence of Parolles does not take

the form of his removal from the society of the play. It is indicative of the nature of comedy, Northrop Frye has observed, that characters who serve to block the integration of the society or the union of the hero and heroine are very often themselves integrated in a show of secure benevolence on the part of the society. Such characters are first reduced to ineffectuality, then admitted to the festivities of concord with which plays of this kind normally conclude. This is what happens to Parolles. He is humiliated, then promises to "repent out the remainder of nature"; he is rejected by Bertram, and finally allowed to join the feast at the end. The reduction of Parolles to a state of impotence is a symbolic act of cleansing in itself. As a result, Bertram and the whole society are freed from his demonism.

In this analysis of *All's Well* I have emphasized the symbolic function of character and action. From such a concentration, the major intention of the play is, I think, revealed. It is a symbolic drama in which a regenerate condition of natural order is reached as a result of both the purification of the whole society of the play, and the initiation of the central characters into a life of mature virtue. It is Helena's function in particular which brings the drama to this regenerative conclusion. The redemptive power of her chastity not only allows her to solve her own personal conflict between the values of Eros and Diana, but it also serves to restore the fictional world through which she moves by reconciling the sensual level of experience with the value of purity originating in the eternal order of the upper world.

The main point which emerges from this kind of approach to *All's Well* is that the conflict of sensuality and chastity in the play, and the subsequent equilibrium between those two forces, is an extensive metaphor for the larger tension between fallen nature and a divine world, and for the interaction between those two realms which ultimately resolves the tension. With the force of chastity most intimately bound to the upper world, and the force of sensuality most intimately bound to the lowest level of nature, the problems of romantic love are capable of carrying this heavier burden of meaning. It is not too much to expect that all the elements of a drama of chaste love have been controlled in order to imitate an embellished, golden, or redeemed natural world; and not simply to tell us poetically that true love is something like salvation. The regeneration of man and the renewal of his world do not function in this play as rhetorical support for the virtuous condition of true love; rather, the virtuous condition of true love functions as a figure for the perfection of the natural order.

Finally, I want to identify the kind of reality imitated in Shakespeare's play, and to clarify my observations by reference to some of the points made by Erich Auerbach in *Mimesis* and Northrop Frye in *Anatomy of Criticism*. There is evidence in the Renaissance of a shift away from an interest in a transcendent order of perfection toward a belief in a divinely arranged order of nature as sufficient ground for the restoration of man and his world. In much Renaissance poetry, including *All's Well*, metaphorical techniques are employed to reveal the immanence of spirit in the natural world rather than to imitate a transcendent spiritual reality. The goal of this form of expression is the poetic representation of nature restored to its proper location just below (and imitative of) the eternal order of the divine world. It is a vision of reality which includes the sensual drives of life in harmonious conjunction with the ideal of eternal purity associated with the world of spirit. That lower part of nature associated with sexuality is not, in this attitude toward reality, totally renounced; it is, rather, cleansed of its corrupting aspects so that passion may take its place in a world animated by sensual as well as ethical forces. Thus, the representation of reality in *All's Well* may be seen as a reflection, both thematically and formally, of a prevailing Renaissance cultural attitude. *Thematically,* it translates into symbolic dramatic action the pervasive Renaissance desire to progress from a fallen to a redeemed natural condition. *Formally,* it maintains analogical relationships —through character, action and imagery—between the natural and the supernatural in order to express the *immanence* of the divine in nature rather than the *transcendence* of nature by the divine.

The intellectual and creative attempts of Western culture to come to terms with the relationship between the natural and the spiritual is, in part, the concern of both *Mimesis* and *Anatomy of Criticism.* Although their approaches are quite different, I think Auerbach and Frye come to some similar conclusions which, in turn, confirm some of the observations made here about *All's Well* and the kind of reality it is a representation of. First of all, Auerbach's metaphors of the vertical and horizontal lines employed in his discussion of the shift from the figural to the secular representation of reality are helpful in defining more precisely the fictional world I have spoken of. The vertical (figural) line signifies a continuity of nature and spirit based on the acceptance of the temporal as well as the eternal, but a continuity in which a divine reality ultimately supersedes (or fulfills) the earthly. In the Renaissance there is a dissolution of this vertical, figural line in the direction of the horizontal or secular, signifying the more thoroughly temporal destiny of human life. As a result of this shift from the figural to the secular, a new conception of the continuity of nature and spirit is required. For poetry this means that a figural representation of reality is no longer possible; but certainly in much Renaissance poetry there is evidence that the figural or transcendental connection between temporal event and its completion in heaven is not so completely dissolved as to remove totally the influence of the world of the divine upon the world of the natural. *All's Well,* for example, presents a fictional world in which neither the supernatural nor the natural claims complete supremacy, although the scene of the action itself is limited to the confines of the natural world. The natural presses its claim in terms of the importance of the experience of passion. The supernatural presses its claim through the necessity of a virtuous and rational natural order originating in the will of God. There is not, in this severely mitigated figural representation of reality, direct poetic imitation of the upper world of spirit; but the influence of that world on nature is revealed through various forms of analogy and allusion, such as those surrounding the figure of Helena which allow Lafeu to recognize a "heavenly effect in an earthly actor."

Northrop Frye's approach is more exclusively formal than Auerbach's, since he deals with "the shape of literature as a whole"; yet the "romantic mode" described in the *Anatomy* is very much like that fictional world which falls between the totally figural and the totally secular. The romantic mode is a literary manner displaced from the "mythic" in the direction of a more plausible representation of reality. Consistent with this movement away from the mythic, the narrative of romance is what Frye calls cyclical rather than dialectic. This means that the narrative action takes place wholly within the mutable, cyclical, seasonal world of nature. However, this cyclical world of the romantic mode borders on, at its extremities, what Frye calls the eternal worlds of the apocalyptic (heaven) and the demonic (hell). At these borderlines the influence of heaven and hell upon the natural world originates; but the interaction is represented only allusively and symbolically, for the characteristics of the romantic mode do not allow the direct imitation of the divine and the demonic. Again, this is a picture of the world of *All's Well;* a world in which the symbols of initiation and purification and the rituals of concord do not introduce a transcendental redemption, but simply gild the brazen world in which the action begins.

These formal characteristics of the romantic mode helpfully classified by Frye, and the cultural significance of the decline of figural thought in the Renaissance outlined by Auerbach, are both relevant, I think, to the form and meaning of *All's Well that*

Ends Well. It is a symbolic drama employing the romantic contention of passion and purity as a figure for the temporal redemption of nature, an image of *concordia mundi.*

IMMORTALITY IN TWO OF MILTON'S ELEGIES

William M. Jones

University of Missouri

Don Cameron Allen[1] and Hugh N. MacLean[2] have both recently offered interesting explications of Milton's early poem "On the Death of a Fair Infant Dying of a Cough." These critics have shown that the poem is much better constructed than has previously been believed. It yet remains to be demonstrated that the poem's thought progression bears a striking resemblance to a much later Latin poem on death: "Epitaphium Damonis." Unlike the Latin poem, this early one does not make use of pastoral conventions. In this respect it is more similar to Milton's epitaphs for the Marchioness of Winchester, the University Carrier, the Bishop of Winchester, and the Beadle of Cambridge. Unlike these non-pastoral poems on death, however, it is concerned with a strictly personal relationship; the subject here and in the pastoral poem is an individual rather than a person known by a title.

Milton's thinking on the subject of the Fair Infant begins quite soundly in the reality of the death. A child, a wind, and the resulting death are all present in the first stanza as he meditates upon the poetic possibilities of the situation. These three basic elements, cause, recipient, and result, are readily transformed into a rather obvious metaphor: the wind that caused the disease and the resulting death are both personified, and the child becomes a flower.

---

[1] *The Harmonious Vision: Studies in Milton's Poetry* (Baltimore: Johns Hopkins University Press, 1954).

[2] "Milton's *Fair Infant*," *ELH*, XXIV (1957), 296–305.

Milton expands this simple comparison between the infant's death and Winter's blighting of a flower by uniting it with classical examples of wind and death. He interpolates his own infant into this mythic world and eventually relates the real child to a specific myth involving death and flower. By the fourth stanza he has arrived at the logically appropriate Apollo-Hyacinth story, which also contains cause, recipient, and result. But here the killer-lover restores the dead to life in the natural world. At the conclusion of this stanza Milton comments specifically on the difference between the infant and Hyacinth. Apollo

> then transform'd him to a purple flower
> Alack that so to change thee winter has no power.

Milton, by integrating his subject with myth, has united the classical flower with the flower he has made of his poetic subject, noting as he accomplishes this fusion that life for his flower cannot be regained. No hope for such a satisfactory metamorphosis exists for the dead child because in the metaphor of the first line Milton has already accomplished poetically what Apollo accomplished in the myth. The classical story simply did not contain for Milton at that time a satisfactory solution to the problem of the dead child.

Consequently, Milton does not stop with the classical example. He looks elsewhere for explanation. The infant's soul, now disembodied from its earlier flower metaphor by the power of the wind, hovers in eternity, while Milton examines throughout three stanzas the eternal form that underlay the mortal appearance of his flower-infant. In this search for the eternal resting place of the infant's spirit, Milton moves again through the areas that the poem has already covered. Once more he begins by assuming that the child was mortal, then suggests that it was, instead, a star, an object of the natural world that also contains the destroying wind, and finally that it was a hiding goddess, a being from the mythic world of Apollo, who used the natural world to achieve reality for dead Hyacinth.

Again, however, this mythic world carries Milton no further than the opening metaphor of the infant flower. Apollo's hyacinth too was subject to the wind's blast. Milton must move beyond the human, natural, and classical mythic that constituted the worlds of the first four stanzas to the world of ethical abstraction (Justice and Truth) and the Christian world of angels ("the golden-winged host"), with which he ceases his questioning.

These questions have recapitulated the entire first portion of the poem and moved beyond to the Christian realm in search of an explanation of the relationship between the temporal and the eternal. These questions are not casually posed, nor is the conclusion hastily reached. The series of questions in the second half of the poem restates in an orderly manner what has been metaphorically presented in the first four stanzas, adding also the ethical and the Christian as possible areas where Milton can find for the infant flower an eternity more satisfactory than a rebirth in nature.

Milton, however, is no more satisfied with "golden-winged hosts" than with the Apollo legend. His final answer to the problem of the infant's death is found neither in the classical myth nor in Christian immortality, but in the actual world from which the actual child was taken. Any other consolation is too theoretical to be immediately satisfactory. In the last stanza Milton suddenly shifts from speaking to the child, whom he first addressed as a flower, then as a disembodied spirit. Now, for the first time, he speaks to the mother. She must give with patience what God has lent. "This if thou do he will an off-spring give/That till the worlds last-end shall make thy name to live." The sorrowing mother is promised fame, not heavenly fame but worldly fame. The fertility of nature is the earthly hope that Milton holds out to Anne Phillips who was already pregnant with another child.

135

The natural fertility of God's world, the fertility that produced the first flower, will give the mother another. In this final stanza the flower image of the first stanza is forsaken for direct statement about the infant and the mother. The mythic is put aside now that it has served its purpose in moving Milton poetically to a conclusion that has validity in the actual with which he began.

This conclusion is to some extent a compromise with reality. $Hyacinth_1$ is not $Hyacinth_2$, nor is $child_1$ $child_2$, but Milton has arrived at a conclusion not uncommon in Elizabethan poetry: the fullness of God's creation provides for more, not the same.[3] Patience is the answer to individual sorrow, and the hope of fame in the future brings a consolation for the living that the mythic and the more popular Christian concept of eternal life cannot effectively produce.

I might add that this same movement out to the mythic and back to the actual is discernible in Lycidas.[4] "Lycidas" begins in the classical (Triton), moves through the natural (Camus) and Christian (St. Peter), and concludes with the new pastures that offer productivity, not to Lycidas but to the sorrowing human who, having examined cause (water), recipient (Lycidas), and result (death), has then resolved the problem of the death by accepting the infinite fertility that God's universe offers ("Tomorrow to fresh woods and pastures new").

In the "Epitaphium Damonis" Milton has prepared for his conclusion about the fertility of the actual world from the very beginning. The shepherd Thyrsis counts the time since Damon's

[3] Edward Hubler has pointed out the relevance of this idea to Shakespeare in "Three Shakespearean Myths: Mutability, Plentitude, and Reputation," *English Institute Essays: 1948* (New York: Columbia University Press, 1949), pp. 95–122.

[4] Cleanth Brooks and John E. Hardy have pointed out the realism of the conclusion to "Lycidas" in *Poems of Mr. John Milton* (New York: Harcourt, Brace, 1951), p. 186.

death by the green stalks and the golden harvest.[5] This poem, more than "The Fair Infant," remains in close touch with reality. There are no searchings in the mythic or specifically Christian for the solution to the problem of death. Even though the poem is presented in pastoral terms, Milton's trip to Italy, his plans for a British note, and the cups which Manso gave are all, either literally or possibly, part of the world Milton knows. At the conclusion, when Milton presents the heavenly name and the human name, he faces the actual world as he did when he addressed Anne Phillips in the last stanza of "The Fair Infant." Damon in heaven is given his true name, Diodati, the name that Milton has always had for him.

In this poem, however, consolation cannot come as it came for Anne Phillips in the hope of a new birth in the natural world. Diodati had no children nor any lasting productions by which men could remember him. Milton now seems to reach for the hope of heaven that he has passed over in favor of natural fertility in the earlier poem. The question of the first part of "Epitaphium Damonis," "But what is to become of me?" also seems to be laid aside; the fertility must be of some kind other than that of Anne Phillips.

Diodati, who has produced nothing to give him lasting fame, participates in a heavenly marriage feast:

> Because the crimson flush of modesty, and youth without stain were your pleasure, because you ne'er tasted the joys of the marriage couch, see, virginal honors are reserved for you.
> With your bright head encircled by a radiant crown, and carrying the gladsome shade of the broad-leaved palm, you will consummate, eternally, immortal nuptials. There

---

[5] "Et jam bis viridi surgebat culmus arista,

  Et totidem flavas numerabant horrea messes."

The translation quoted throughout is that of Charles Knapp, *The Works of John Milton* (New York: Columbia University Press, 1931), I, i, 294–317.

is singing, where the lyre revels madly, mingled with choirs beatific, and festal orgies run riot, in bacchante fashion, with the thyrsus of Zion.[6]

More subtly than in any other of his poems on death, the movement here is again from heavenly to actual. The thyrsus of Zion has its basis in the actual world just as much as Anne Phillips' fertility has its basis here. Milton seems to accept the orthodox hope of heavenly bliss, but by paralleling in the last stanza the heavenly name Diodati with the earthly one Damon, Milton encourages the reader of the poem to see for himself that the parallel extends beyond the explicitly stated. If Damon's name in heaven is Diodati, then the lamenting shepherd's name in heaven must logically be Milton. In heaven, however, both names are known; therefore, when Diodati-Damon participates in a marriage feast which includes the touch of the thyrsus of Zion, there is room in the heavenly celebration for Milton-Thyrsis too.

Before he wrote the "Epitaphium Damonis," Milton had used the name Thyrsis twice, in "L'Allegro" and again in "Comus." The Attendant Spirit in "Comus" took this name when he assumed an earthly disguise. Milton had not, of course, created the name; Vergil had introduced it into the pastoral tradition. Milton's choice of this particular name, however, was not accidental. With his knowledge of Greek, he certainly recognized it as the proper noun made from the root of the "thyrsus" word. In "Comus" the thyrsus-related character represents protective

---

[6] "Quod tibi purpureus pudor, & sine labe juventus
    Grata fuit, quod nulla tori libata voluptas,
    En etiam tibi virginei servantur honores;
    Ipse caput nitidum cinctus rutilante corona,
    Letaque frondentis gestans umbracula palmae
    Aeternum perages immortales hymenaeos;
    Cantus ubi, choreisque furit lyra mista beatis,
    Festa Sionaeo bacchantur & Orgia Thyrso."

creativity as opposed to the wilder revels of Comus, the actual son of Bacchus and Circe.

When Milton uses the same name again six years later, it has a similar, but more refined, function. The green stalks of the opening passage echo throughout the poem and reappear in the fertility symbol of the heavenly staff. But this staff, lifted in heaven to touch the virgin Diodati, has an earthly counterpart, Milton. The thyrsus of Zion, raised in heaven, produces a reaction on earth.

Milton has faced reality firmly throughout this poem and has decided that he, as the earthly servant of the thyrsus, will fulfill the friendship in earthly terms. Although it is God's thyrsus at the marriage feast that blesses Diodati with eternal fruitfulness, for Milton the consolation is not primarily a heavenly one, but an earthly one, similar to that arrived at in the fertility promise to Anne Phillips. The seemingly forgotten question of the early part of the poem, "What will happen to Thyrsis?," is answered. He will serve as God's fertilizing power and produce a piece of literature, which Milton elsewhere defines as "the image of God," "that ethereal and fifth essence, the breath of reason itself . . . , an immortality rather than a life" (*Areopagitica*).

In the epitaph he wrote as a boy and in the epitaph he wrote as a mature man he reveals the same basic attitude toward death. In spite of the promise of heavenly reward the individual man accepts the reality of death and works within that reality toward fulfillment of earthly possibilities. Anne Phillips must accept the essentially irreconcilable loss of one child in the hope of future children. Milton must accept the loss of a friend and meditate patiently upon the fertility which he, as a bearer of heavenly power, has received. True fame may have its root in heavenly soil, but it is achieved in this world. The Christian promise, like the classical metamorphosis, remains too unreal and illusory for Milton's own practical needs. In "The Fair Infant" Milton began his search for the meaning of death in the reality of the dead child, moved through the natural world and the classical to the Christian and returned finally to the only consolation that he could find emotionally satisfying: productivity is assurance of fame to the world's end. The "Epitaphium Damonis" reaches the same conclusion, but the consolation is more surely known from the beginning of the poem. The symbols are built in, not in a search, but in a knowledge that maturity in the world comes from right use of human possibility. And the thyrsus of Zion, like the potential of Anne Phillips, sees its actual embodiment in Thyrsis who will, through human creativity, gain eternity if "my beloved Thames, before all others, and the Tamura [the Tamar], swart with metals, and the Orcades in the furthermost billows learn my song." In similar fashion previous generations of Renaissance thinkers, guided by secular reason, had pronounced upon the nature of true eternity. Magnifico Giuliano in *The Courtier,* discoursing on the productive cycle of human life, had said a century earlier: "Thus nature, moving as it were in a circle, completes the figure of eternity and in such a way gives immortality to mortals."[7]

In *De Doctrina* Milton might bring forth a number of lucid arguments in favor of the resurrection of the dead; but in these two poems about people he had known well, he seems to have accepted the limitations of the life in the flesh. Try as he might to find another answer, he never can progress emotionally beyond the initial image of earthly productivity that he found in the Apollo-hyacinth myth of his first youthful attempt in "The Fair Infant."

[7] Baldassare Castiglione, *The Book of the Courtier,* trans. Charles Singleton (Garden City, New York: Doubleday, 1959), p. 216.

OF RUSKIN'S GARDENS

Charles T. Dougherty
Saint Louis University

It is a commonplace that Ruskin's career underwent some kind of change around 1858. This change is often described as a shift from an interest in art to an interest in economics, but a glance at his bibliography will demonstrate that this is not what happened. Except for his public letters, Ruskin wrote very little on economics; he never stopped writing about art, and no matter whether Ruskin wrote of art or of economics, his subjects were always harmony and love, and their opposites, chaos and pride. They are, for him, the intellectual and moral poles of human action in any sphere.

There are, however, two works written after 1858 that are radically different from anything else he ever did. These are the final volume of *Modern Painters,* published in 1860, and *Sesame and Lilies,* published in 1865. Of *Modern Painters,* Joan Evans wrote, "But at the very end it returns to Turner, and once with a strange Apocalyptic passage harder to interpret than any picture Turner ever painted."[1] In this work and in *Sesame and Lilies* Ruskin raised his concepts of harmony and love to apocalyptic proportions and universalized and concretized them in archetypical symbols.

In the four years that passed between the publication of *Modern Painters IV,* in 1856, and the final volume, two events occurred which seem to have caused this radical alteration of the course of Ruskin's thinking. He spent the years 1857–1858 arranging, cataloguing, and preparing notes on the Turner Bequest at the National Gallery; and in 1858 he formally renounced his

---

[1] *John Ruskin* (New York: Oxford University Press, 1954), p. 247.

Calvinist and Evangelical heritage. It is a new and different mind which produced the work of the 1860's.

It is true that back in 1841, two years before the publication of the first volume of *Modern Painters,* Ruskin had written the fascinating parable, *The King of the Golden River,* which embodies within its simple story the germ of everything he was ever to write. But this was a plaything, improvised to amuse a little girl, and it was ten years before he reluctantly permitted its publication, in 1851. With the exception of this work, the allegorical vein in Ruskin's thought remained submerged until the events of 1857–1858 brought it dramatically to the surface. The opportunity to go over at one time the whole sweep of Turner's work, some nineteen thousand sketches, fifteen years after the defense of Turner had been begun, was bound to give Ruskin new understanding and to modify his early judgments. It was this experience plus the formal rejection of his inherited, conservative religious beliefs in the same year, coupled with the renewed contact with the archetypical figures of Turner, that seems to have released a torrent of speculation that had been dammed up in him for all those years. *Modern Painters V* and *Sesame and Lilies* were written by a man possessed of an apocalyptic vision of art and the universe that can only be compared with that of Milton or of William Blake.

As he restudied the pictures of Turner, two symbols began to dominate Ruskin's consciousness—the garden and the woman. The garden, of course, had been the root myth of *The King of the Golden River.* This fairy tale about a fertile valley which, because of greed and liberal economics, became a desert and was made fertile again by love and charity had been written for a little girl whom he later married. She grew up and left him and married Millais; and Ruskin had just begun to give drawing lessons to a new little girl, Rose LaTouche, who was to absorb his affections during the next decade. There is a biographical as well as an archetypical relationship between Ruskin's gardens and his girls. Consequently, as we read *Modern Painters V* and watch the growth of Ruskin's conception of harmony, we also see his woman gather to herself the qualities of Juno, Athena, the Madonna, Andromeda, the Rhine maidens, and the Faërie Queene, and finally emerge as one aspect of the Word made flesh—the risen Christ. The garden takes on rich symbolic value as the living, harmonious alternative to the wasteland; and the two symbols complement each other as the woman becomes the guardian of the garden and the implacable enemy of the serpent who covets it. The last two parts of *Modern Painters V,* with the exotic chapter headings: The Law of Help, the Dark Mirror, The Lance of Pallas, The Wings of the Lion, The Nereid's Guard, The Hesperid Ægle, catch Ruskin's vision of a universe in which chaos is victor over harmony, the desert and the sea over the garden, the serpent over the woman, and death over life. "Of Kings' Treasuries" is an account of a fallen world, "Of Queens' Gardens" is a prescription for the redemption of that world, and *Modern Painters V* is the key to the vision.

When Ruskin began his public career with the publication of *The Poetry of Architecture* in 1837, he thought of harmony in the eighteenth-century sense of the "picturesque." The concept grew until it merged with the prevalent conservative social, economic, and political thinking that was marked by a horror of anarchy and a hunger for order. But even before Matthew Arnold gave the whole complex notion its classic expression in *Culture and Anarchy* in 1869, Ruskin had broken through that parochial and national view. By 1860 he had come to see the chaotic liberal, democratic world as a manifestation of the Fall, and he saw every bit of harmony, at any level, even a single work of art, as a precious manifestation of the Redemption.

A poet is not a "maker" in the sense of a craftsman or artificer, but in a far higher sense. "A poet, or creator, is ... a person who puts things together, not as a watchmaker steel, or a shoe-

143

maker leather, but who puts life into them" (VII, 215).[2] This power of creation, which Ruskin calls invention, is a visible sign of Divine or immortal life in man,". . . that which is deathful being anarchic or disobedient, and that which is divine ruling and obedient; this being the true distinction between flesh and spirit" (VII, 215n). "Government and co-operation are in all things and eternally the laws of life. Anarchy and competition, eternally, and in all things, the laws of death" (VII, 207). This drastic dichotomy between the forces of death and the forces of life is carried into the economic order most forcibly in *Unto This Last,* also published in 1860.

The garden, in *Modern Painters V* and in *Sesame and Lilies,* is the Garden of Eden, the unfallen world, or the redeemed world. The former work opens with an account of how man has lost Eden, and how he can regain it: ". . . the Flaming Sword will still turn every way, and the gates of Eden remain barred close enough, till we have sheathed the sharper flame of our own passions, and broken down the closer gates of our own hearts" (VII, 14). The volume closes in the same vein. Between there is a discussion of the fallen world which Turner painted. For, in Ruskin's view, Turner's greatness lay in the fact that he painted it truly; his weakness lay in the fact that he had no hope of its redemption. Turner's first major work (1806) was "The Garden of the Hesperides." In this picture the nymphs of Hesperides are watched over by a dragon. Ruskin devotes several pages to an exhaustive analysis of the symbolism of these figures at various levels. In general this dragon is "the demon of all evil passions connected with covetousness; that is to say, essentially of fraud, rage, and gloom" (VII, 401). He is looking down upon the wealth of the earth, which is watched over by the singing nymphs. At another level he is the wind of the

[2] All references are to *The Works of John Ruskin,* ed. E. T. Cook and Alexander Wedderburn (London: George Allen, 1903–12).

desert and the power of the sea gazing wrathfully upon the garden. This dragon is the Satan of Genesis (what Ruskin calls "other books of Genesis than Hesiod's"), and the Mammon of Milton.

Ruskin had already examined a series of pictures which developed the devil and the woman theme. He had studied the figure of the ruined angel contrasted to the female Melancholia in Dürer's "Knight and Death," and a similar scene in Claude's "St. George and the Dragon." In his view the great achievement of the Greeks was the goddess Athena, and he felt that the Venetians' noblest conception of man was the female figure, and of divinity was the Madonna. This constant balance between the serpent and the woman is a symbol at the core of Ruskin's vision. Of Turner's "The Garden of the Hesperides," he writes:

> Such then is our English painter's first great religious picture; and exponent of our English faith. A sad-coloured work . . . in a sulphurous hue, as relating to a paradise of smoke. That power, it appears, on the hill-top, is our British Madonna; whom, reverently, the English devotional painter must paint, thus enthroned, with nimbus about the gracious head. Our Madonna,—or our Jupiter on Olympus,—or, perhaps, more accurately still, our unknown god, sea-born, with the cliffs, not of Cyrene, but of England, for his altar, and no chance of any Mars' Hill proclamation concerning him, "whom therefore ye ignorantly worship."

> This is no irony. The fact is verily so. The greatest man of our England, in the first half of the nineteenth century, in the strength and hope of his youth, perceives this to be the thing he has to tell us of the utmost moment, connected with the spiritual world. In each city and country of past time, the master-minds had to declare the chief worship which lay at the nation's heart; to define it; adorn it; show the range and authority of it. Thus in

Athens, we have the triumph of Pallas; and in Venice the Assumption of the Virgin; here, in England, is our great spiritual fact for ever interpreted to us—the Assumption of the Dragon. No St. George any more to be heard of; no more dragon-slaying possible: this child, born on St. George's Day, can only make manifest the dragon, not slay him, sea-serpent as he is; whom the English Andromeda, not fearing, takes for her lord. The fairy English Queen once thought to command the waves, but it is the sea-dragon now who commands her valleys; of old the Angel of the Sea ministered to them, but now the Serpent of the Sea; where once flowed their clear springs now spreads the black Cocytus pool; and the fair blooming of the Hesperid meadows fades into ashes beneath the Nereid's Guard.

Yes, Albert of Nuremberg; the time has at last come. Another nation has arisen in the strength of its Black anger; and another hand has pourtrayed the spirit of its toil. Crowned with fire, and with the wings of the bat. [VII, 407–8]

I believe that Ruskin is saying something like this: The greatness of Venice was built upon a religion which is false. Venice made a garden of the sea, and she called upon the Angel of the sea to protect her. The divinity of the Venetians was the Madonna, and their worship of her was pure and good. She is the very type of what was greatest in Venetian art, for she was assumed into heaven, body and soul. But the religion of the Venetians was false, the Angel of the Sea was really the Serpent of the Sea, and when the sea and the worm devoured their work the Venetians vanished as the rainbow.

England is the new Venice. She too thought to make the sea her garden, but while making a smoking inferno of her fields, the dragon of Covetousness rose up from the sea, and England embraced him. The dragon has captured the Faërie Queene and there is no Arthur to rescue her.

146

Five years after the Hesperides picture, Turner painted another on a similar subject. "Another dragon—this time not triumphant, but in death-pang, the Python slain by Apollo. Not in a garden, this slaying, but in a hollow, among wildest rocks, beside a stagnant pool" (VII, 409). Python is a more terrible foe than the Hesperides' dragon. He only guarded the treasures of the earth; Python is "The Corrupter," he is "the worm of eternal decay" (VII, 420). "Apollo's contest with him is the strife of purity with pollution; of life with forgetfulness; of love, with the grave" (VII, 420). Apollo is the lord of life (VII, 277), he is the helpful God, associated thus with harmony (VII, 215). This picture, "Apollo and the Python," is a representation of the victory of life over death.

There is a world, Ruskin believed, which God loves, and which Christ lights. This one assuredly is not it. Hence this is no world. This is Chaos. The Light of the World taught His children to pray "Thy kingdom come." It is the prayer for light, for harmony, for creation itself to come to the earth-begotten, to the "Chaos children" (VII, 458).

> But it is still at our choice; the simoom-dragon may still be served if we will, in the fiery desert, or else God walking in the garden, at cool of day.... The choice is no vague nor doubtful one. High on the desert mountain, full descried, sits throned the tempter, with his old promise— the kingdoms of this world, and the glory of them. [VII, 459–60]

It is the choice between the wasteland, whose lord is Death, and the garden, whose lord is Christ. Ruskin is saying in the last chapter of *Modern Painters V* what he said in the first chapter, that we can return to the Garden of Paradise whenever we want to. But in Ruskin's final vision the worm is not slain by the sword, but by the love of Christ. This choice is also what *Sesame and Lilies* is about: "Have you not sought Him often...

sought Him in vain at the gate of that old garden where the fiery sword is set? He is never there; but at the gate of *this* garden He is waiting always..." (XVIII, 144).

England is a ruined garden, which has been turned into a coal mine.

> Suppose you had each... a garden, large enough for your children to play in... no more—and that you could not change your abode; but that, if you chose, you could double your income, or quadruple it, by digging a coal shaft in the middle of the lawn, and turning the flower-beds into heaps of coke. Would you do it? I hope not....
> Yet this is what you are doing with all England.
> [XVIII, 133–4]

Sesame and Lilies can be understood at the first level by equating the King with intellect and the Queen with the feelings. From *Modern Painters I* forward, Ruskin is concerned with Truth as the object of intellectual perception, and with Beauty as the object of what was variously called "the feelings," "moral perceptions," or "the affections." Thus the good woman portrayed for us in "Of Queens' Gardens" is partly the traditional "Angel in the House," or Dickens' Esther Summerson generalized; she is partly an admonishment to Rose, who was showing disturbing signs of growing up; and she is partly an expression of the general intuitive bias that is a mark of the Victorian mind.

Ruskin had explained the complex tradition of the woman as the guardian of the riches of the earth in "The Nereid's Guard":

> And was it not well to trust to such keepers the guarding of the golden fruit which the earth gave to Juno at her marriage? Not fruit only: fruit on the tree, given by the earth, the great mother, to Juno (female power), at her marriage with Jupiter, or *ruling* manly power (distinguished from the tried and *agonizing* strength of Hercules). I call Juno, briefly, female power. She is, especially, the

goddess presiding over marriage, regarding the woman as the mistress of a household. Vesta (the goddess of the hearth), with Ceres, and Venus, are variously dominant over marriage, as the fulfilment of love; but Juno is pre-eminently the housewives' goddess. She therefore represents, in her character, whatever good or evil may result from female ambition, or desire of power: and, as to a housewife, the earth presents its golden fruit to her, which she gives to two kinds of guardians. The wealth of the earth, as the source of household peace and plenty, is watched by the singing nymphs—the Hesperides. But, as the source of household sorrow and desolation, it is watched by the Dragon. [VII, 394–6]

This guardianship was also the role of Eve and we recall that while Athena, the Madonna, and Melancholia watched over the Greeks, the Venetians, and the world of Dürer, in England Andromeda had embraced the dragon, and the Faërie Queene was held a captive. In "Of Queens' Gardens" the queens are also captives: "you shut yourselves within your park walls and garden gates; and you are content to know that there is beyond them a whole world in wilderness..." (XVIII, 140).

In *Sesame and Lilies* the King's highest achievement is wisdom, which is likened to gold. We have seen before the important distinction between anarchy and harmony, which is the difference between death and life. However there are two kinds of order: "Life and consistency, then, both expressing one character (namely, helpfulness of a higher or lower order)..." (VII, 206). Gold is an example of this lower order of helpfulness, for it is found in any inanimate substance. "Orderly adherence, the best help its atoms can give, constitutes the nobleness of such substance" (VII, 206). Gold is a type of this adherence, and it is the highest harmony the King can achieve.

The plant is the type of the higher order of helpfulness.

149

"The power which causes the several portions of the plant to help each other, we call life" (VII, 205).

As the intellect is to the heart, as gold is to the lily, as wisdom is to charity, as the Old Testament is to the New, is the king's treasury to the queen's garden. Yet there is an imaginative difficulty in this work that stems from the fact that Ruskin's woman ultimately is a Christ-figure. We have seen that Apollo is the slayer of the serpent, and we know also that it is a woman's heel which is to crush the head of the serpent. There is an ambiguity in this relationship which is to grow more pronounced: Apollo-Mother, Arthur-Gloriana, Perseus-Andromeda, Christ-Madonna. It issues in the identification of the Queen and the risen Christ. She is the Queen of Peace. He was known by the breaking of the bread, and earlier, by distributing it to the multitude. Now it is the Lady who "communicates" (XVIII, 138) the bread, not to the Master Himself, but to "the least of these." And the bread which she distributes is not "bread made of that old enchanted Arabian grain, the Sesame, which opens doors;— doors not of robbers', but of Kings', Treasuries" (XVIII, 105). The bread she offers is the Bread of Life which was distributed to the disciples at Emmaus, and the gate she opens is the gate of the Garden of Eden. Christ is the gardener who appeared to Madeleine, and who sowed good seed in his field. Thus we may say that the role of the woman (or of the female principle) in the world is to perform the acts by which the risen Christ showed himself to man. It is in woman, "born to be Love visible" (XVIII, 128), that the Word is made flesh in our days.

It is safe to assume that the King whom Ruskin has especially in mind is Solomon. He had been the subject of "Qui Judicatis Terram," and in "The Wings of the Lion" Ruskin had discussed Veronese's "Presentation of the Queen of Sheba." The King's treasury is wisdom, and its type is gold. The Queen's garden is life, and its type is the lily. Solomon had achieved the peak of human treasure and of human wisdom before the

Redemption, but not even Solomon in all his glory was arrayed like one of these!

In the third lecture, "Of the Mystery of Life and its Arts," Ruskin turned to our wisest men, to Dante, Milton, Homer, and Shakespeare, in the hope that one of them could justify the ways of God to man. None of them, he asserts, can give us the answer which we seek, for theirs is the wisdom of the chaos world. It has been revealed to us that we shall be judged on how we fed and clothed and housed "the least of these," so, instead of reading, this is what we must be about. The General Judgment is now.

> Is there but one day of judgment? Why, for us every day is a day of judgment—every day is a Dies Irae, and writes its irrevocable verdict in the flame of its West. Think you that judgment waits till the doors of the grave are opened? It waits at the doors of your houses—it waits at the corners of your streets; we are in the midst of judgment.... [XVIII, 180]

Redemption is to be found not in gold or in wisdom, but in charity; not in the King's Treasuries but in the Queens' Gardens.

The next year, Ruskin published *The Queen of the Air,* which is an attempt to get behind these sophisticated later myths in whose framework he had been writing, to reach back to the primitive myth, and finally to the thing itself—the natural root of the myth. This work was to occupy him as he embarked in 1870 on his Slade Professorship.

MYTH AND SYMBOL IN CRITICISM OF FAULKNER'S "THE BEAR"

Alexander C. Kern

State University of Iowa

What things are meant by myth and symbol in the criticism of "The Bear?" When Ike McCaslin leaves behind not only his gun but also his watch and compass, before he is able to see Old Ben, the bear of the story, for the first time, this has been taken to represent a rite of passage and a mystical experience.[1] The bear himself has been interpreted both as a totemic creature and as an Ishtar figure in a myth of Ike's rebirth.[2] When Sam Fathers, a sort of priest who initiates Ike into the rites of the forest, greets a great buck as "Chief, . . . Grandfather," and Ike later so addresses a menacing rattlesnake, the latter has been described as a totem.[3] Moreover, Isaac's consciousness that he has, like his biblical namesake, narrowly escaped immolation, and his further consciousness that he became a carpenter because that calling was good enough for the Nazarene, have been referred to the Judeo-Christian tradition.[4] Finally, when Ike at the end of the story comes in a clearing upon the tree full of whirling squirrels, prevented from escaping by a desperate Boon at the foot of the

[1] Kenneth LaBudde, "Cultural Primitivism in William Faulkner's 'The Bear,'" *American Quarterly*, II (1950), 325; Otis B. Wheeler, "Faulkner's Wilderness," *American Literature*, XXXI (1959), 29.

[2] John Leydenberg, "Nature Myth in Faulkner's 'The Bear,'" *American Literature*, XXIV (1952), 70; and Richard J. Stonesifer, "Faulkner's 'The Bear': a Note on Structure," *College English*, XXIII (1961), 219–220.

[3] Carvel Collins, "A Note on the Conclusion of 'The Bear,'" *Faulkner Studies*, II (1954), 58–60.

[4] Olga Vickery, *The Novels of William Faulkner* (Baton Rouge: Louisiana State University Press, 1959), p. 131; Hyatt Waggoner, *William Faulkner* (Lexington: University of Kentucky Press, 1959), pp. 203, 207.

trunk, this has been suggested as a mandala.[5] While all these examples imply a background of religion, there is another level of material which has also been called myth. Faulkner's allusions to the career of Daniel Boone, to the pattern of Cooper's Leatherstocking, to the concept of Thomas Bangs Thorpe's "The Big Bear of Arkansas,"[6] and to the destruction of the wilderness at the time (according to Frederick Jackson Turner) of the close of the frontier: all these indicate a consciousness of secular material which has gone into mythical readings of the American experience.

I wish for purposes of analysis to distinguish between primitive, Christian, and American myth, although they all become one, when considered aesthetically as intellectual constructions that fuse concept and emotion into images;[7] or when considered psychologically as primordial patterns which arise from the collective unconscious of the race and so mysteriously move us when they appear in literary works;[8] or perhaps when considered anthropologically as pragmatic charters of primitive faith and moral wisdom.[9] Since I am closer to the empirical orientation of such anthropologists as Malinowski and Kroeber and DuBois than to the idealistic pattern of psychoanalytical critics like Jung and Neumann, I will concentrate on what is known about Chickasaw customs, Christian symbolism, and the American myth in my attempt to interpret "The Bear."

---

[5] Carvel Collins, "Are These Mandalas?" *Literature and Psychology,* III (1953), 3–6.

[6] William Van O'Connor, *The Tangled Fire of William Faulkner* (Minneapolis: University of Minnesota Press, 1954), p. 129n.

[7] Henry Nash Smith, *Virgin Land* (Cambridge: Harvard University Press, 1950), p. vi.

[8] Erich Neumann, *The Great Mother,* trans. by R. Manheim (New York: Pantheon, 1955), pp. 3–4.

[9] Bronislaw Malinowski, *Magic, Science and Religion and Other Essays* (Glencoe, Ill.: The Free Press, 1948), p. 79.

This is a task which is difficult enough to offer a significant challenge. For one thing Faulkner is not an easy author; in fact he is so complex that it has required a whole generation of scholars and critics to begin to approach a consensus as to his meaning, and no one can hope to be completely correct. For another, "The Bear" was composed over a period of at least seven years and consequently shows clear marks of the development of Faulkner's ethical and aesthetic aims, which I have worked out elsewhere. And finally, Faulkner employs myth very self-consciously, enriching his story by allusions to mythical materials without intending to carry over their complete allegorical meanings. So, taking my courage into my hands, I endeavor to expound some of the more significant sets of symbols in "The Bear."

Permit me to anticipate my conclusions. The first three parts of this five-part tale dealing with the education of Ike McCaslin in the ethic of the forest by Sam Fathers, the son of a Chickasaw Indian chief, and by Old Ben, the bear, emphasize Indian rites and attitudes. The fifth part, which is closely connected with the first three, includes an epiphany and introduces a key Christian symbol, the snake. Part four, which takes place after part five and was the last section written, turns to Ike's place in a "Christian" society, shows Ike renouncing his plantation as a result of what he has learned in the wild, and is more heavily dominated by Christian symbolism. The whole constitutes the profoundest and most penetrating exploration to date of the American myths of the destruction of the Eden of the wilderness and the fate of the Adamic hero. For me the inclusion of part four creates the greatness of the story, moving as it does in terms of plot from romance to realism and in terms of the hero from idealization to humanizing irony.

The pattern of "The Bear" is that of the romance in Professor Northrop Frye's "Theory of Myths," with certain significant ironic inversions and displacements. To quote: "The complete form of the romance is clearly the successful quest, and such a completed form has three main stages: the perilous journey . . . ; the crucial struggle, . . . and the exaltation of the hero. . . . The central form of the romance is dialectical: everything is focused on a conflict between the hero and his enemy, and all the reader's values are bound up with the hero. Hence the hero of romance is analogous to the mythical Messiah or deliverer. . . . " And Frye goes on to say that the ideal Christian pattern is that of St. George who kills the dragon which is identified with both serpent and leviathan. That is, the romance is a form in which myth is reduced to substantially human terms.[10] This makes sense when properly interpreted, which means that the scheme is somehow inverted. First, the bear is not really the evil leviathanlike destroyer. Old Ben's relationship to Moby-Dick is here significant, for neither is inherently evil. It is Ahab who piles all evil on the white whale's hump, while it is Major DeSpain who wrongly attributes to the bear the destruction wrought by Lion. Old Ben is made a symbol for the wilderness which carries mainly affirmative values. And this explains why Ike, the technical hero, does not kill the bear, and why having been taught by Old Ben and Sam Fathers, he renounces his inherited land.

Parts one, two, three, and five contain a good deal of Indian ritual which I wish to compare with what ethnologists know about Chickasaw culture to see how Faulkner is manipulating primitive myth into symbol. So I will consider the three animals that can be referred to as totems: the bear, the buck, and the snake. I will in part dispose of the bear as a candidate now, but since the story is called "The Bear" and he is clearly important, I will have to return to him later in the paper. Swanton, the basic authority on this tribe, notes that the Chickasaws had a totemic clan organization with a deer clan, but according to the

---

[10] Northrop Frye, *Anatomy of Criticism* (Princeton: Princeton University Press, 1957), pp. 187–189.

best though incomplete information had no bear or snake totem.[11]

If Faulkner knew his ethnology, this would eliminate the bear as totem, and whatever Faulkner says of the Chickasaw is consistent with the work of Speck and Swanton. For instance, the Chickasaws ordinarily inhume a corpse under his house but, according to Adair, "When any of them die at a distance, . . . they place the corpse on a scaffold, covered with notched logs to secure it from being torn by wild beasts or fowl of prey; when they imagine the flesh is consumed and the bones are thoroughly dried, they return to the place, bring them home, and inter them in a very solemn manner."[12] Such knowledge could account for Sam's burial at the end of part three.

On the other hand general bear lore which has been recorded by Hallowell[13] is conspicuously omitted. Faulkner makes no use of the idea of hibernation which was so mysterious to primitive man and so thoroughly connected the bear with the underworld and rebirth that as Rhys Carpenter analyzes the myth, Odysseus, who went to the lower world, was really the son of a bear.[14] Nevertheless, the slaughter of the bear by means of a knife, which is consistent, goes no further to indicate it is a totem.

If the bear is not a totem—and this does not prevent his greater role as symbol of the wilderness—what about the deer as totem? Here I think the case is strong. The deer was one of the totem animals held by the Chickasaws to be the ancestor of a sib or clan. So it is at least consistent with the tribal pattern that Sam Fathers addresses the great buck of "The Old People"

[11] J. R. Swanton, "Social and Religious Beliefs and Usages of the Chickasaw Indians," *Annual Report, Bureau of American Ethnology*, XLIV (1928), 192.

[12] Quoted by Swanton (see note 11, above), p. 229.

[13] A. I. Hallowell, *Bear Ceremonialism in the Northern Hemisphere* (Philadelphia: University of Pennsylvania Press, 1926), passim.

[14] Rhys Carpenter, *Folk Tale, Fiction and Saga in the Homeric Epics* (Berkeley and Los Angeles: University of California Press, 1946), p. 128.

156

as a reputed forefather and totemic object when he raises his hand and says, "Chief, . . . Grandfather."[15]

Of course I am overstating a little when claiming that Faulkner's use of totem fits all known facts. While the Chickasaws were a hunting tribe organized in clans, which are the essential conditions for totemism, they were, like the Creeks and Choctaws, matrilineal. But since Sam's mother was a quadroon she could not account for his membership in any particular totemic group. Yet insofar as Sam was an Indian, he would have a ritual animal. And insofar as Ike McCaslin is Sam Fathers' spiritual son, he would have a different totem. Faulkner plays this pattern with a brilliant invention which links the primitive hunting section with the modern plantation portion of his tale. When, in part five, Isaac encounters the threatening rattlesnake (in a revised portion not in the original tale "Lion") and addresses it automatically in the old tongue, " 'Chief,' he said: 'Grandfather,' " he is seen as Sam's son but with a difference, for the snake is no Chickasaw totem. But it is a major Judeo-Christian symbol, as is indicated by the language about it: "the ancient and accursed about the earth, fatal and solitary . . . evocative of all knowledge and an old weariness and of parish-hood and of death." This reading is confirmed by Faulkner's external statement that "the snake is the old grandfather, the old fallen angel, the unregenerate immortal."[16] So Ike, if he is not accepting the evil in nature, is certainly saying that he is a grandson of Carrothers McCaslin, a son of the Christian world, and not the complete inheritor of the wilderness ethic. Recognizing his descent from the symbolic snake, instead of remaining in the country or moving to Sam's hut in the woods, he goes to Jeffer-

---

[15] William Faulkner, *Go Down Moses* (New York: Modern Library, 1955), p. 184.

[16] Frederick Gwynn and Joseph Blotner, ed., *Faulkner at the University* (Charlottesville: University of Virginia Press, 1959), p. 2.

son. Despite several statements by scholars[17] that he returns to the wild when he surrenders the plantation, he really moves to town to live, and spends only hunting vacations in the gradually contracting wilderness.

This return to the Christian world in part four is symbolized by the use of heavy concentration of biblical reference, sometimes used simply as symbol. When, for example, Isaac refers to his name as indicating that like his namesake he narrowly escaped immolation, Faulkner is putting to good use the fortuitous fact that the name came from one of the author's old hunting companions and was at first applied to another character.[18] And Ike's imitation of Christ, which internal evidence shows was one of Faulkner's final additions, is used in a similarly referential way, for Ike is no *pharmakos* or sacrificial animal who assumes the sins of the world. He is in part seeking escape, as Cass says, but is no savior and cannot even totally save himself.[19] He recognizes that no one is completely free, a fact which Faulkner indicates by Ike's inability to accept the consequences of miscegenation even when it involves love, as it does in "Delta Autumn." This reference to Jesus the man as opposed to the Christ is of course characteristic of Faulkner's mind and work.

Ike's constant reference to the Bible on his twenty-first birthday in his long dialogue with Cass tends strongly to balance and I think negate the view that Ike is a romantic nature mystic of an Emersonian sort.[20] There is a goodly amount of Calvinism in Ike, whether of Presbyterian or Miltonic derivation. For one thing, God is for him the creator of the world and hence no

[17] Vickery (see note 4, above), p. 134.

[18] Robert Coughlan, *The Private World of William Faulkner* (New York: Harper, 1954), p. 97.

[19] Ursula Brumm, "Wilderness and Civilization: a Note on William Faulkner," *Partisan Review*, XXII (1955), 347.

[20] Irving D. Blum, "The Parallel Philosophy of Emerson's *Nature* and Faulkner's *The Bear*," *Emerson Society Quarterly*, No. 13 (1958), 22–25.

pantheistic immanence. For another, Ike is constantly aware of God's foreknowledge of man's failure, though man is free to choose. But God has still a plan and there will be others even if Ike himself cannot succeed. Such hope as "The Bear" presents, and there is more than at the end of the earlier books, lies in the doctrine of a chosen few. This means that the future will be like the past, with individuals struggling but getting only a little better, because man's humanity since the fall makes him subject to failure; and means that there will be no millennium on this present earth.

Examination of "The Bear" does not convince me that Faulkner is a primitivist.[21] The wilderness was gone by Faulkner's day and he regrets the fact. But it is a mistake to think that everything, in the author's eyes, has gone to pot since the institution of settled agriculture, private property, and even chattel slavery has superseded hunting. His interest in the human struggle is more important than nostalgia for the past. Were this not the case, he would never have found it necessary to write part four of "The Bear." In the other sections Ike is pretty much the subconscious-wish-fulfilling hero of romance, but he is forced to turn to the thorny, problematical and imperfect world, of which we are ourselves a part. Faulkner not only inverted the archetypal Christian myth by making Ben good and having a bumbling Boon slay the bear, but also returned Ike to a sinful world. So romance is given a twist of realism and the hero is reduced to life size once again. R. W. B. Lewis, who in a series of seminal essays, from parts of which all later interpretations can have grown, denies that Faulkner is the kind of primitivist who holds that the best men are those closest to nature, for Ike expressly rejects the idea. Ike knows that America is not "the second, last chance for humanity," because he is aware of original sin, which the

[21] Leydenberg (see note 2, above) and LaBudde (see note 1, above) both make Faulkner a primitivist.

settlers brought with them in their ships. This knowledge frees him from the danger of innocence and permits him to develop a conscience, so that the primitive is transcended into the ideal.[22] What James Baird defines technically as primitivism is very useful here. In his book *Ishmael* he argues that a cultural failure of Christianity forced many writers to employ material from primitive religions as symbols for their visions of life, and this use he calls primitivism. Baird of course points out that the authors need not hold the primitive rites as efficacious nor the myths as true.[23] Certainly Faulkner does not; but he probably does not hold the Christian story to be true either, for he more than once refers to the Jewish "fairy tale" which was imposed upon the Western world.[24] And this enabled Faulkner to employ both Chickasaw and Christian myth and symbol in his remarkable summation of the American past. But this is not primitivism in any usual sense.

Now to return to the figure of the bear once more. The critic who sees Old Ben as an Ishtar figure from which Ike is reborn insists on omitting part four. This is important because the Ishtar idea is suggested through the mystic number seven by claiming that each of the other parts has seven episodes and throwing out part four which has more and so does not fit.[25] Despite Faulkner's own later statement that part four belongs to the novel *Go Down*

[22] R. W. B. Lewis, "The Hero in the New World: William Faulkner's 'The Bear,'" *Kenyon Review,* XIII (1951), 641–660; *The American Adam* (Chicago: University of Chicago Press, 1955), p. 199; *The Picaresque Saint* (London: Gollancz, 1960), pp. 206–207. Cf. Herbert A. Perluck, "The Heart's Driving Complexity: An Unromantic Reading of Faulkner's 'The Bear,'" *Accent,* XX (1960), 23–46, for the opposing ironical position.

[23] James Baird, *Ishmael* (Baltimore: Johns Hopkins University Press, 1956), pp. 6, 16.

[24] William Faulkner, *New Orleans Sketches* (New York: Grove, 1961), p. 54; *Go Down Moses,* p. 291.

[25] Stonesifer (see note 2, above), pp. 220–221.

Moses and not to the story "The Bear,"[26] part four is stubbornly there. So I would say rebirth, yes, but why Ishtar?

Whether there is a mandala at the end of "The Bear" I do not know, but I think sense can be made of the more obvious elements. When the reader has come through the anguished rhetoric of Ike's discovery of the family injustice and incest and his subsequent though compromising surrender of the cursed land, he is equipped to see this concluding experience as a kind of insight or recognition which marks a point of moral decision in Ike's life. The encounters with the snake and with Boon Hogganbeck at the end make sense. The former I have already explained as a recognition and acceptance of evil as part of the human condition. Boon Hogganbeck's punning name also has significance. He is both Daniel Boone as the slayer of the bear, and hog as the desperate claimant of all that is left of the wilderness—the squirrels, those pitiful survivors of man's unthinking rapacity. So Ike recognizes that the forest of Sam Fathers and Old Ben is wrecked, and that all that is left is to return to society to live a life of self-denying sacrifice, but also one of sterile isolation. And the symbols for these must be weighed against the mandala of psychological integration, which for me is the less dominant note.

Indeed I am convinced that Ike's imperfection is part of the final effect of "The Bear." For while Ike is neither a romantic hero nor a tragic protagonist, Faulkner here takes a tragic view of history in which the doom of the wilderness is foreknown and inevitable, and the best efforts of the best men are not enough to gain a victory over evil or themselves. Yet Faulkner here affirms the importance of men like Ike McCaslin, who is able to learn from Sam Fathers and Old Ben the pride and humility, the courage and restraint, which he puts into practice as carpenter and occasional master of the hunt.

[26] *Faulkner at the University*, p. 4.

THE *DE VULGARI ELOQUENTIA* AND DANTE'S QUASI AFTER-LIFE

Warman Welliver
Butler University

Dante's absorbing interest, his vocation, in the decade before he was thirty-eight years old seems to have been politics. Like many literate aristocrats, though more successfully than most, he wrote lyric poetry. Still, his calling was not poetry but politics.

In the years 1301–1303 his political career ended abruptly. First he was exiled from Florence when Pope Boniface's French soldiers and Florentine partisans overthrew the government of his party. Then his and his fellow exiles' attempt to fight their way back went badly and Dante abandoned the others in disgust. After the day in late 1301 when he left Florence as an envoy to Rome charged with the responsibility of trying to dissuade the Pope from his aggressive designs, he never re-entered the city.

When Dante abandoned the exiles' campaign against Florence in 1303, he turned to prose. In the next five years he wrote two doctrinal treatises, the *De Vulgari Eloquentia* and *Convivio*. After that he began the *Divine Comedy*. In this essay I am going to outline a novel interpretation of the *De Vulgari Eloquentia* and then, using that as a guide, speculate on the nature and origin of Dante's post-exilic program of writing which culminated in the *Divine Comedy*.[1]

The following interpretation of the *Eloquentia* is novel in that it is allegorical. I do not find that anyone has previously treated the work as anything other than literal doctrine. Treated

---

[1] For a more detailed analysis of Dante's prose and its relation to the *Divine Comedy* see Welliver, *Questions of Intent* (Indianapolis: Clio Press, 1961), pp. 43–82 (cited hereafter as *QI*).

as literal doctrine the work presents many stubborn difficulties.[2] Treated as an allegory the difficulties can be resolved. It seems reasonable enough, moreover, to suspect the operation of the poetic imagination in anything written by so great a poet as Dante and, in particular, to look for allegory in any work of a poet so prone to allegorical expression.

The *Eloquentia* consists of two books. Book One consists essentially of two parts, first, the history of spoken language from Adam to fourteenth-century Italy, and secondly, Dante's quest, discovery, and celebration of what he calls the illustrious Italian vernacular. This essay on language amounts to a linguistic tragedy and a linguistic comedy joined and balanced with utmost symmetry. God created a perfect exemplar of language to be spoken by Adam. Nimrod, the arrogant hunter-king, dared in his pride to build the Tower of Babel, and men lost their perfect tongue. They scattered abroad and multiplied their languages until in Italy alone over a thousand varieties were spoken. Not only was unity lost but quality as well. The vile, misshapen, cacophonous dialects of Italy which Dante surveys, are at the opposite pole from the noble language of Adam (*DVE*, I, 1–10).

But precisely at the middle of Book One, the nadir of linguistic tragedy, an omen of comedy appears. We suddenly find that Dante is on the trail of the one perfect Italian language. Gradually he turns back the tide of multiplicity by eliminating the dialects of Italy from consideration one by one. Then, by a miracle of deductive reasoning, he regains linguistic perfection. Just as one is the measure of all number and white of all color, so there exists one perfect Italian language which is the measure of all Italian vernaculars and which is reflected in all of them though it is identical with none. Linguistic paradise thus regained, Book One ends with a long panegyric on this perfect Italian tongue (*DVE*, I, 11–19).

[2] *QI*, pp. 48; 125, n. 67.

Look back for a moment at the actors in this little drama of language. Obviously the villain in the tragedy is Nimrod; he committed the original linguistic sin and after him language is corruptible and mortal. His counterpart, the hero in the comedy, is Dante, and the symmetry between them is underlined by Dante's savage hunt for the perfect language in the forest of ugly Italian tongues and by his vituperative and sneering manner. He has cast himself in the role of a perverted redeemer of Nimrod's original sin, the insolent hunter repairing the damage done by the insolent hunter-king.

But his self-dramatization does not end there. The master of the original perfect language, the man first blessed with it, was Adam. The master of linguistic Paradise regained, the man on whom this illustrious language confers such prestige and happiness that, as he says, his exile does not concern him in the least, is Dante. He is not only the anti-Nimrod; he is the new Adam in a new Paradise of language. The man who has just been crushed in real life has contrived a rather spectacular triumph for himself in his imagination.

He has yet to substantiate his claims, however, for in his panegyric on his perfect Italian language there is not a word of Italian. He has somehow to cope with the concrete problem of just what this perfect Italian is. That is presumably one function of Book Two, and Dante lists six questions concerning his language which he now intends to answer (*DVE*, I, 19).

In the first three chapters of Book Two he deftly disposes of the first three questions. Who is worthy to use this language? The greatest poets. What material is worthy to be treated in it? Love, arms and virtue. In what form should the treatment be cast? In the poetic form of the *canzone*. But in chapter four comes trouble. The first sign of it is so faint that the unsuspecting literal mind can gloss it over altogether. "Quando quidem aporiavimus extricantes. . . ." Dante begins, and this ought to mean, following the usual and scriptural and etymological note of trouble in *aporio*,

164

"Now that I have gotten into trouble disentangling [the answers to these first three questions] . . ." But the literal mind, which is averse to trouble, looks the other way and assumes that Dante simply meant he had been working very hard at answering his first three questions, in spite of the fact that there is no sign of excessive toil in those three chapters.[3]

Aporiavimus is soon followed by unmistakable signs of trouble, however. We find at once that question number three has not been disposed of after all, as we had assumed at the end of chapter three. Before we can go on to the fourth question, we have to get to the bottom of this matter of the *canzone,* says Dante. Next he stumbles into outright misrepresentation. "Looking back over what I have said, I recall that I have several times given the name of poets to those who write verses in the vernacular tongue." Looking back over what he has said, I cannot find a single instance where he has used the name of poets for versifiers in the vernacular. Even so, he insists on his misrepresentation. "What's more, I have had good reasons for daring to use this word *poetas.*" In the very manner of his persistence in error, he gets into more trouble. He says neither "I have had good reasons to dare to *dicere* this word *poetas,*" nor, using the verb he has just used, "I have had good reasons to dare to *vocare* them *poetas.*" Instead he says, "I have had good reasons to dare to *eructare* this word *poetas.*" *Caveat lector!*

Next he introduces for the first time the idea of tragedy, as he decrees that the *canzone* must be written in the tragic style. Then he concludes chapter four with a disordered, ill-tempered, and ominous paragraph on the extreme difficulty of being a great poet. *Hoc opus et labor est,* he says, and one can hardly miss the ominous context of these words in the *Aeneid;* to go down to Hades, to get into trouble, this is easy, but to get out, that is

---

[3] Dante, *De Vulgari Eloquentia,* ed. A. Marigo (Florence: Le Monnier, 1948) pp. 147, 320.

toil and travail. Next, claiming to quote Vergil, he misquotes him, just as he has shortly before misquoted himself. Finally he lapses into his first invective since the low point of Book One where he was castigating the brutish Italian vernaculars.

As Dante proceeds with his project of getting to the bottom of the *canzone,* we soon find that he has turned aside from his original program into a confused, pedantic and crotchety digression.[4] The rest of Book Two, and therefore of the work, is an almost uninterrupted crescendo of trouble which reaches a climax in the last chapter. *Aporiavimus* turns out to have been fair warning and a true omen. Leaving out the crescendo, let us look at the climax of the trouble.

"Let us inquire," says Dante in the last chapter, "into the proper length of the stanza of a *canzone.* Since in all poetry we express either a favorable or an unfavorable attitude—for example, we may wish to persuade or dissuade, to congratulate or ridicule, to praise or express contempt—let those words which are unfavorable always at the end hurry, and let the others proceed with seemly discursiveness gradually to a conclusion." This is the conclusion of the *De Vulgari Eloquentia.*

As an exercise in raising many questions and answering none, this response to the question, how long should the stanza of a *canzone* be, is positively delphic. Passing over the quibble that the rule does not unequivocally answer the question about length, let us assume, as the literal mind does assume, that the rule is a rule for the length of stanze. As such it raises two difficulties which the literal mind has found insurmountable.[5] It seems to say that critical sentiments should be expressed in short stanze and laudatory in long stanze. Rigid convention required, however, that all stanze in any single *canzone* should be of equal length. How, then, could a poet following Dante's rule change

---

[4] "disgressionis nostre," II, 6.
[5] Marigo (see note 3, above), pp. 276–277.

from critical to laudatory sentiments, or vice versa, in the same *canzone*, as he might very well wish to do? Following Dante's rule he would have to vary the length of his *stanze*, but this would be a violation of inviolable convention. Therefore he would find himself unable to change from critical to laudatory sentiments, or vice versa, and, if he had started out lamenting, would be condemned to lament to the bitter end. Secondly, Dante's own *canzoni* appear to follow precisely the reverse of this rule for the length of *stanze*; his critical *canzoni* favor a long stanza, his laudatory a short. The rule is not only impractical; it does not even conform to the practice of the poet who prescribed it. But Dante was unable to find anything better, concludes the literal mind, and abandoned the unfinished *Eloquentia* in disgust.

The allegorical attitude comes to this final crisis in a different mood from the literal, however, for it has followed the constant multiplication of trouble ever since the start of the long digression. It suspects, therefore, that this harsh impasse is the last crashing chord in a tragic sonata. The absurd rule, the abrupt ending, half the program left hanging, are these not a perfect climax of the long crescendo of troubles? And doesn't even the absurd rule find its own grotesque application and justification in the very debâcle which it marks? It says, in effect, that once a poet embarks on an unfavorable course, there is no turning back. Isn't this precisely what Dante demonstrates here? He took the path of trouble away from his smoothly unfolding program and now there is no turning back. Artfully he has contrived his own downfall and has contrived to fall saying that from the first misstep he was condemned to fall. Just as Book One was a carefully devised triumph, Book Two, and therefore the whole work, proves at the end to be a carefully devised defeat and humiliation.

Why did he do this to himself? Notice how closely the unfolding of Book Two parallels the unfolding of Dante's political downfall. In the middle of his life and career he was suddenly forced to deal with the threat of the Papacy and its French army to him and his city; in the middle of the program for his treatise, "before I migrate to other things," as he pointedly remarks, he is suddenly forced to break off and shift his attention to some intractable material of which there has been no notice in his program. As the trouble threatened his city more seriously, he had to go to Rome on a diplomatic mission, had to make, as it were, a *digressio* to Rome; his departure from the middle of his program of discussion proves to be a long digression. It takes little imagination to picture what troubles he must have had in his negotiations with Pope Boniface VIII; his digression from the program of his treatise is replete with troubles. After weeks of fruitless argument at Rome, the news of the catastrophe struck him and he was powerless to return to Florence; at the far end of his digression, after chapters of confused and ill-tempered hairsplitting, he struck down his work with the rule that the poet cannot return and left his argument forever exiled from the program from which it had wandered. The allegorical attitude concludes that the design of the *Eloquentia* is an effigy of Dante's personal tragedy.

Now the way in which an effigy is made and used tells more about the person devising it than about the person imaged. As Dante shapes the history of language and the rules of poetics into a rehearsal of his own recent tragedy, he is really revealing his present character. Obsessed with the injustice and indignity visited on him, he is lacerating his wound. Insolent, vindictive, scornful, and deceitful, he is lashing back at the world which is tormenting him.

This is an ugly sight, and it is hard to escape the feeling that there is something intensely evil about it. To twist the story of God's language and the canons of art into one's own cry of anguish and hate, is a diabolical undertaking. Recalling that at the start of Dante's fatal digression he posted the advice which the sybil gave to Aeneas at the start of his descent to Hades, one asks, was this man not metaphorically in Hell as he wrote this work? Are not his insolence and vindictiveness, his rage and deceit, the traits of the justly damned? Is not this work a kind of fusing of his present violent temper with the ultimate fate which awaits so evil a temper?

If Dante was suffering the mortal equivalent of Hell as he wrote the *Eloquentia,* then this strongly implies, in the case of so systematically allegorical a poet as he, that he had recently experienced the mortal equivalent of death. It seems obvious from his constant preoccupation with his banishment, not only in the *Eloquentia* which immediately followed it but ever afterward, that it must have been that tragic event which soon became a metaphor of dying. After his exile he was as a dead man, though still alive. As he wrote the *Eloquentia* in rage and vindictiveness, he was as a soul tortured in Hell.

There is, however, one crucial difference between Hell in the imagination and the real thing. The latter is said to be eternal; from the former, as Vergil says, some few living men by God's grace escape.[6] There are several signs that the *Convivio,* the work which Dante undertook immediately after the *Eloquentia,* corresponds to a laborious passage through Purgatory. He begins with a labored apology which, as he puts it, purges the "bread" of his prose of impurities. In contrast to his triumph and then downfall in the *Eloquentia,* he introduces himself in the *Convivio* as "an ignoble wanderer, almost a beggar" cast off by his fellow men and then laboriously succeeds in reaching, by the end of the work, a definition and illustration of nobility which vanquishes all others. As he plods through his interminable and barren disquisitions, he is as a soul toiling through Purgatory toward salvation. At the end the feigned incompleteness of the *Convivio* is sweet, solemn, and ascendant, like the unforeseen ascent of souls from Purgatory to Paradise, rather than harsh and abrupt as in the *Eloquentia.*[7] His next work, the *Divine Comedy,* he wrote

---

[6] *DVE,* II, 4; *Aeneid,* VI, 126 ff.

[7] For a more detailed discussion of the *Convivio* see *QI,* pp. 56–69.

from the vantage point of salvation and a revelation of Paradise. From his banishment through the *Eloquentia, Convivio* and *Divine Comedy* he was living a metaphorical journey from death through Hell, Purgatory and Paradise.

Seen in this way these three works reveal an extraordinary unity of conception. Their continuity, the intricate harmony and correspondences among them, the myriad passages which reflect forward in anticipation of something in a later work or backward in recollection of something in an earlier, all seem to imply that by the beginning of the *Eloquentia* in 1303 Dante had formulated the main outlines of a complete and complex program of writing which was to carry him to the end of the *Paradiso* around 1319. Let one example suffice of the kind of foresight I mean. At the beginning of the *Eloquentia,* the infernal and crudely deceitful work, Dante makes several statements about the language which Adam spoke. When Dante meets Adam near the end of the *Paradiso,* Adam too makes several statements about that same language.[8] Everything Dante says through Adam, directly contradicts what he had said in the *Eloquentia,* just as Paradise contradicts Hell. What he says in the *Paradiso,* moreover, illustrates the very theme of the *Paradiso* which the *Eloquentia* had in effect denied, that man is free to speak and create as he will. From signs like this it seems evident that when Dante began the *Eloquentia* in 1303, he already had a very fair idea of the *Paradiso.*

Yet if this bold and intricate program of writing was based on Dante's metaphorical journey through the after-life, it could hardly have been conceived before his fall from power in 1301–1302, for that event was the quasi death which plunged him into the emotional abyss which he recognized and exploited as a quasi after-life. He must have hammered out this marvel of creative imagination in the tense and troubled two years or so

[8] *DVE*, I, 4–6; *Paradiso*, XXVI, 103–142.

between the fall of his party at Florence and the beginning of the *De Vulgari Eloquentia*.[9] This post-exilic program of writing, the execution of which was to preoccupy him for most of the rest of his life, involved a radical change in his vocation. He decided to abandon politics and embrace writing (though of course he still dabbled in politics when opportunity offered, just as before he had dabbled in writing). In the trilogy of works which Dante's program envisaged, there is a good deal of material for reconstructing the thought of those two years which led to his decision to embrace a life of writing and which dictated the shape and contents of his program.

We have seen that an analogy with the crucial future events of man's life, namely his death and after-life, provided Dante with one principle of design for his program. There are indications that an analogy between Dante's experience and two crucial events in man's past provided him with much of the inspiration and resolution to embrace his new life. The most crucial historical event of universal significance on which he looked back was the life, death and destiny of Jesus. The prototype of that event was the life of Israel in Egypt and its exodus in search of the promised land. In both cases God required of his favored people a painful sacrifice in order to attain a glorious end. In agony of soul and body they were thrust from their native homes to win the promised land. The suspicion that he too might be one of God's most favored people can never have escaped Dante for long. He too was thrust from his home in agony. The conclusion of the syllogism was clear. He too was marked for the promised land. What was *his* promised land to be? He was to write the greatest poem, a poem which would show men with all the

---

[9] I say this notwithstanding the fact that the last chapter of the *Vita Nuova* clearly contains a resolution to write the *Divine Comedy*. For the reasons given in *QI*, pp. 104–109, I believe that that resolution and some other passages were not in the *Vita Nuova* before Dante's banishment.

authority of God's sanction the way to salvation. He had been crushed as a petty statesman that he might arise and conquer as a universal poet. Those are the two crucial events of his life on which the *Divine Comedy* repeatedly dwells. He will be cast into exile; he will live with all posterity as one of the greatest of poets. By analogy with the stories of Israel and Christ he was able to transmute his tragedy, the loss of his home and the end of his political life, into God's providential offer of a new life and a lasting triumph.

Not only did God's Providence, communicated by analogy between Dante's situation and past events, lead him to his new life of writing and show him its ultimate goal; it also suggested the medium in which he should prepare to achieve that goal. Beatrice, his first and spiritual love, had died. Then he had loved, quite unspiritually, the *donna gentile.* Then somehow Beatrice beatified had found him again. Likewise he had loved Florence and it too had been snatched away. Then he turned on it, quite unspiritually, and tried to fight his way back. Then somehow political life beatified, the dream of the Holy Roman Empire, found him and rescued him from his sordid brawling. Was not the implication for his writing crystal clear? So far he had written small-scale love poetry. He was destined to write transcendent and universal poetry. Was he not meant to get from the one to the other by turning on the love poetry and abusing it, by killing and mortifying its spirit, as he had abused the memory of Beatrice and turned on Florence? So he plunged into an orgy of anti-poetic prose—the pedantic Latin poetics of the *Eloquentia,* the interminable dissection of his poems in the *Convivio.*

But though these were both anti-poetic, they differed, as I have suggested, in that they were written under the signs of Hell and Purgatory. Having plumbed the depths of arrogance and hatred and deceit in the *Eloquentia,* Dante could begin the constructive anti-poetry of the *Convivio.* In it he came to terms with God's will (as of course he had already decided he must), accepted his apparent tragedy as the sign of his promised triumph, and finished his metamorphosis from the angry exile to the universal poet. Having completed the *Convivio,* he was at last crowned and mitred to describe God's Providence in transcendent poetry.

Presumably he had long foreseen how this was to be done. Prompted by Providence he had journeyed through his prose metaphors of Hell and Purgatory, fusing his own changing nature with its changing fate. Now, having reached emotional salvation, he retraced his steps in memory and imagination and poetry. The metaphor of the anti-poetry became the drama of the poetry. The realms of the after-life and of God's Providence through which he had struggled toward salvation, he now peopled with others, whose earthly natures he fused with their ultimate fate as he had fused his own in the prose. The drama was so convincing because, among other reasons, he had already lived it himself.[10]

[10] For a somewhat similar interpretation of the *Divine Comedy* by a scholar who did not recognize the applicability of his interpretation to the doctrinal prose, see Erich Auerbach, *Dante: Poet of the Secular World,* trans. Ralph Manheim (Chicago: University of Chicago Press, 1961). I am much indebted to this book, which I had not read before writing *QI,* for helping me to clarify the relation of the prose works to the *Divine Comedy.*

THE GOLDEN BOUGH: IMPACT AND ARCHETYPE

John B. Vickery
Purdue University

Now that it has figured in Raymond Chandler detective stories, Harper Prize novels (*Tower in the West* by Frank Norris), and serious minor fiction like *Devil by the Tail* or *The City of Trembling Leaves* as well as the more central works of the age, no one would deny, I imagine, the scope of *The Golden Bough's* impact. Not only is it the most encyclopaedic treatment of primitive life available to the English-speaking world but it is the one that lies behind the bulk of current literary interest in the subject of myth and ritual. But what may not be so obvious are the reasons for Frazer's classic having become, in Professor Buckley's words, "an almost inexhaustible source book for the central myth and symbols of a twentieth century literature."[1] In effect, these reasons are partly factual, partly historical, and partly literary.

By factual reasons I mean those concepts ingrained in both *The Golden Bough* and the climate of opinion of the late nineteenth and early twentieth centuries. Both in *The Golden Bough* and the age the movements of these notions were charted by a compass whose cardinal points were the concepts of rationality, fertility, irrationality, and sterility. The major topics explored were sex, superstition, and survival (an alliterative if not particularly novel triad). Frazer's detached chronicling of the phallic nature of primitive cults was—whether he would admit it or not—

---

[1] Jerome H. Buckley, *The Victorian Temper* (Cambridge, Mass.: Harvard University Press, 1951), p. 245.

the anthropological equivalent of Freud's plumbing of modern man's sexual impulses. Both too were intrigued by the way in which, as Frazer remarked, "the sexual instinct has moulded the religious consciousness of our race (VII, viii).[2] And while Frazer gave scant credence to theories of the unconscious and steadfastly refused to read Freud, nevertheless, he too contributed to the twentieth century's mapping of the levels and modes of human consciousness. *The Golden Bough* is crowded with illustrations that are virtually dramatic analyses of prophetic foresight, shamanistic trances, mass psychology, and the denial of common sense categories of thought. Like *Being and Nothingness* it merges psychology and the concrete scene of fiction, but in an infinitely more readable form.

Out of these mental phenomena Frazer derived key concepts which reveal his affinities with those other seminal minds of the age, Marx and Darwin. While he never really grasped the economic dimensions of primitive society in anything like their real complexity, he was able to seize on one salient fact about human institutions such as religion, government, private property, and marriage. Implicitly in *The Golden Bough* and more openly in *Psyche's Task,* he shows that man's motives and arguments for his actions are quite other than what he asserts. Like Marx, he analyzes the functional character of institutions as the product of pragmatic and superstitious forces. And though the differences between the two men are considerable, yet it is possible from our present vantage point to see fundamental similarities in their impact on their time. Each showed his readers by a massive accumulation of evidence precisely how much of what has hitherto been thought about mankind and his history could no longer be credited. And more. Each found the explanation of this

---

[2] Sir James Frazer, *The Golden Bough,* 3rd ed. (London: Macmillan, 1911–1915). Frazer quotations are identified in the text by volume and page number of this edition.

mistake in a complex of superstition, self-aggrandizement, and historical necessity.

Important as these notions were in their several ways to Freud, Marx, and Frazer, the really crucial issue and concept was the struggle for survival propounded in the Victorian age and enacted with unparalleled opulence and variety in the twentieth century. While Darwin, Freud, and Marx were framing the issue in biological, psychological, and socio-economic terms, Frazer was developing his own dialectic of myth and reality. For his primitive subjects the struggle for survival is twofold. On the one hand, there is the loosely Darwinian and Marxian aspect provided by attacks from rival tribes or nations and the attrition of drought and starvation coupled with rulers who repress by economic demands, social traditions, and religious appeals. On the other hand, what might be called the Freudian dimension of psychological projections such as myths and deities also figures prominently in the struggle. Frazer's ancient peoples seek to survive as well by myths of divine assistance and rites in which perfect performance assures divine conquest over enemies and hence human survival. In effect, Frazer mediates between the external and internal worlds of Marx or Darwin and Freud, as he himself reveals when he remarks that "to the preservation of the species the reproductive faculties are no less essential than the nutritive." And in so doing, he shows that the individual and the land are the twin foci of man's endless battle for a viable existence, themes which have been as inexhaustible for modern literature as they have imperative for modern life.

Creative artists, of course, had been predisposed toward Frazer's topics by Hardy with his interest in folklore and the peasant mind, by Kipling and Conrad who explored the impact of an alien culture and climate on man, and by Doughty, T. E. Lawrence, and Cunninghame Graham who sensed the human affinities beneath the obvious cultural differences and so emphasized the intelligibility and value of customs and beliefs at first sight strange and barbarous. But even apart from this, much of Frazer's material matched the writers' own interests only set in an unusual context and approached from a new angle. Thus, Eliot's and Miss Sitwell's interest in the religious impulse and its origins is exhaustively catered to by *The Golden Bough* as is Joyce's fascination with elaborate correspondences and the recurrence of certain figures and experiences. The same is true of Yeats's and Charles Williams' interest in magic, Robert Graves's penchant for rational explanations of apparently pointless rites and stories, and Lawrence's stress upon a frank recognition of sexual impulses.

Though the obscure and strange material of *The Golden Bough* was engrossing in its own right, Frazer's volume would not likely have had so great an influence on literature had it not appeared at a remarkably propitious historical moment. For one thing, it marked the culmination in subject and method of a long line of development extending back at least to the eighteenth century. (William Robertson Smith, Frazer's mentor and friend, identified the beginning of the Cambridge school of comparative religion with John Spencer and his *De Legibus Hebraeorum Ritualibus et earum Rationibus* of 1685.) Frazer's interest in the nature and interrelations of religion, myth, cult, and ritual was a continuation of the work of such men as Hume, Herder, Heyne, Creuzer, Mannhardt, Tylor, and Robertson Smith. Similarly, the comparative method—to which he adhered throughout his lifetime—was the product of many hands, most notably Lafitau, Montesquieu, de Brosses, Pitt-Rivers, Maine, Darwin, and Tylor. Thus, *The Golden Bough,* apart from its own intrinsic merits, represented the flowering of a school of anthropology rather than the founding of a new movement. For the so-called evolutionary school originated as early as the 1860's and achieved its greatest influence around 1910 when the third edition of Frazer's classic was coming off the presses. By appearing in its most complete form when it did, *The Golden Bough* not only gained a ready-made audience predisposed towards its subject, method, and attitude but also escaped being overwhelmed by the views of Franz Boas which were destined to dominate virtually the entire field of anthropology in one way or another and which exerted their full effects from about 1925.

Significant as content and publication date are for the literary impact of *The Golden Bough,* nevertheless they leave us with an unanswered question. Why should it have been Frazer's study rather than some work in anthropology and comparative religion that shaped modern English and American literature? Why, for instance, did not L. R. Farnell's *The Cults of the Greek States* or A. B. Cook's *Zeus,* volumes equally encyclopaedic and equally packed with ancient lore, acquire the same kind of status in the literary world? The content of all three is much of a piece and all were published in roughly the same decade. The explanation, then, must lie in what I have called the literary reason. Essentially, this reason has three major and interrelated aspects: the style, structure, and genre of *The Golden Bough.*

Since they stand in a diminishing order of obviousness, I shall begin with the first, that which sees Frazer's style as contributory to his literary importance. The Latinate diction, the judicious employment of periodic sentences, the eloquent peroration, the handling of sustained analogies, the apposite allusions, the leisurely development of paragraphs, all stamp *The Golden Bough* as a magnificently sustained example of the grand style and of what Sir Herbert Read has called the central tradition of English prose.[3] And though it is obviously not the dominant style of the twentieth century, it is clearly the only appropriate rhetorical mode for that study which Frazer himself called "an epic of humanity."[4] In describing Sir James as "a very great master of

[3] Herbert Read, *English Prose Style* (New York: Pantheon Books, 1952), pp. 186, 191–193.

[4] Quoted by R. A. Downie, Frazer's private secretary, in *James George Frazer* (London: Watts and Co., 1940), p. 21.

art,"[5] T. S. Eliot was concurring with Edmund Gosse's judgment that Frazer's volumes were among those whose "form is as precious as their matter."[6] And when one recalls the elaborate word patterns of "The Dead" or the touching conclusion of *Finnegans Wake,* the luminous and unhurried narrative of Sir Osbert Sitwell, or the bravura flourishes that heighten the travel accounts of his brother Sacheverell, it is apparent that they and *The Golden Bough* have more than a little in common. Similarly, T. S. Eliot's best prose reveals the same quality he finds in Frazer's work, a carefully adjusted combination of the tentative and the precise. Indeed, when Mr. Eliot distinguishes Frazer from Shaw and Hardy as possessing a leaner and more disillusioned sensibility whose rhythm is vibrant with the suffering of the life of the spirit, the affinities with his own work become unmistakable.

In addition, *The Golden Bough* possessed another quality that many writers in the twentieth century were to champion as a notable virtue and a cornerstone of a contemporary style. T. S. Eliot, Ezra Pound, H. D., and Ernest Hemingway—to mention only the obvious names—each stressed in his own way the importance of concreteness, of presenting the external world in all sensuous immediacy as a visual presence. They tended, by a kind of Lockian metaphor, to identify visual and intellectual clarity. Thus, Pound even went so far as to insist on Frazer's importance to "contemporary clear thinking" as well as to "the *art of getting meaning into words*"[7] (italics his). And while they might have felt that Frazer was too inclined to the "purple pas-

[5] T. S. Eliot, "A Prediction in Regard to Three English Authors," *Vanity Fair*, XXXI, 6 (February, 1924), 29, 98.

[6] Quoted by Downie (see note 4, above), p. 110.

[7] Ezra Pound, *Literary Essays* (Norfolk, Conn.: New Directions, 1954), p. 32. Frazer's contribution to abstract speculation is usually treated lightly, but Gilbert Ryle has suggested recently that his work was a stimulus to "the theoretical imbroglios" of twentieth-century philosophy. See *The Revolution in Philosophy* (London, 1956), p. 3.

sage" and the set descriptive piece, nevertheless it is difficult to see how they could have avoided praising his images of the waste land near the Dead Sea or the garden-like regions of Ibreez:

> Ibreez itself is embowered in the verdure of orchards, walnuts, and vines. It stands at the mouth of a deep ravine enclosed by great precipices of red rock. . . . With its cool bracing air, its mass of verdure, its magnificent stream of pure ice-cold water—so grateful in the burning heat of summer—and its wide stretch of fertile land, the valley may well have been the residence of an ancient prince or high-priest, who desired to testify by this monument his devotion and gratitude to the god. The seat of this royal or priestly potentate may have been at Cybistra, the modern Eregli, now a decayed and miserable place straggling amid orchards and gardens full of luxuriant groves of walnut, poplar, willow, mulberry, and oak. The place is a paradise of birds. Here the thrush and the nightingale sing full-throated, the hoopoe waves his crested top-knot, the bright-hued woodpeckers flit from bough to bough, and the swifts dart screaming by hundreds through the air. Yet a little way off, beyond the beneficent influence of the springs and streams, all is desolation—in summer an arid waste broken by great marshes and wide patches of salt, in winter a broad sheet of stagnant water, which as it dries up with the growing heat of the sun exhales a poisonous malaria. To the west, as far as the eye can see, stretches the endless expanse of the dreary Lycaonian plain barren, treeless, and solitary, till it fades into the blue distance, or is bounded afar off by abrupt ranges of jagged volcanic mountains, on which in sunshiny weather the shadows of the clouds rest, purple and soft as velvet. [V, 121–123]

Frazer as much as the imagist or realist put precise details to an imaginative use which produced a subtle, profound, and immediate effect. And not the least of the effects produced by the just mentioned waste land and garden images was T. S. Eliot's borrowing of them for *The Waste Land.*

If Frazer's style in *The Golden Bough* was a genuine literary achievement, one to be ranked with that of Gibbon, even closer connections can be found between its structure and the major works of modern literature. For though at first sight, *The Golden Bough* appears a soberly conservative narrative in the nineteenth century manner, it possesses structural properties that might well attract artists eager for experiments in form. Frazer deliberately avoided a strictly logical and systematic arrangement of his facts and chose instead "a more artistic mould" with which "to attract readers" (I, viii). Hence, the priest of Nemi and his rites open the book since, though not intrinsically important, they provide a simple and easily grasped image of actions and beliefs whose mystery is gradually illuminated as the more important and complex dying gods are introduced and their functions explored. As a consequence, the form of *The Golden Bough* has been likened to that of a strict sonata.[8] While it would be futile to argue for it as a direct source, one cannot help noting the parallel here to the interest in musical form shown by T. S. Eliot in the *Four Quartets,* Conrad Aiken in *The Divine Pilgrim,* James Joyce in *Finnegans Wake* (notably Book II, section iv), Thomas Mann in *Doctor Faustus,* and Edith Sitwell in *Façade* and some of the *Bucolic Comedies.*

Frazer himself, however, thought of his book in pictorial terms. The priest at Nemi is said to be "in the forefront of the picture" while the background is crowded with priest-kings, scapegoats, dying gods, magicians, and fertility deities (I, viii). Indeed, there is a sense in which Frazer, like Yeats, writes under the stimulus of an actual painting, developing its implications in his own fashion and interpreting its significance. According to

[8] H. N. Brailsford, "'The Golden Bough,'" *The New Statesman and Nation,* XXI (May 17, 1941), 502.

Frazer, the full beauty of Turner's painting of Nemi can be felt only when Macaulay's verse account of its ritual has been explained. Thus, the frontispiece and initial epigraph of *The Golden Bough* encompass its central theme. Small wonder he should speak of his book in terms of "sinuous outline" and "its play of alternate light and shadow,"[9] or that on its very first page he should urge his readers to form "an accurate picture" of Nemi (I, 1). Like Yeats and Auden, he plays the pictorial and the verbal off against one another and so achieves their mutual illumination; like Eliot, Pound, and Wyndham Lewis, he carries the visual principle of the artist into literature; and like Lawrence and Virginia Woolf, he attends to even as he creates the emotional vibrations in the object and setting. Nor in the light of this are we surprised to find the late Professor Chew likening *The Golden Bough* to the vision seen by Saint Anthony and the Frazerian images and figures to the nightmarish fantasies of Bruegel or Bosch.[10]

The musical and pictorial similarities between Frazer's study and modern poetry and fiction, though striking and suggestive, are essentially analogies, lines of parallel development. What they indicate most sharply is the extent to which Frazer's structural techniques adumbrate those of some of the major artists of the twentieth century. The question of influence—if it enters at all—operates almost exclusively below the threshold of consciousness. A somewhat stronger case of influence as well as a partial explanation of the attractions of *The Golden Bough* is its non-chronological method of narration. This method results in a work whose structure is shaped by most of the devices that characaterize modern literature. Consider what we may call *The Golden Bough's* macroscopic form. Here is a work dealing with a vast subject which orders its material thematically; which juxta-

---

[9] Quoted by Downie (see note 4, above), p. 21.
[10] S. C. Chew, "Nemi and the Golden Bough," *North American Review*, CCXVIII (1923), 816.

poses conflicting evidence and scenes for dramatic purposes; which presents its point of view by indirect and oblique means; which sees human existence as a flow of recurring experiences; which employs repetition and restatement as emotive as well as intellectual devices; which creates symbolic epitomes of human history out of apparently limited and simple actions; and which makes a unified whole out of a plethora of disparate scenes and topics by an intricate set of allusions and references backwards and forwards in the narrative. Without in the least denying the other contributory forces, one may legitimately suggest that *The Golden Bough* is also, in a very real measure, responsible for the form and shape of modern literature.

In *The Waste Land, The Cantos, The Bridge,* and *Patterson* the thematic ordering of material, the dissolving perspectives, the panoramic sweep, the mingling of the profound and the trivial, the poignant and the bizarre are the same techniques employed in *The Golden Bough*. Similarly, one has but to think of Joyce to see the extent to which contemporary literature, like Frazer, conveys its point of view through selection of details and arrangement of scenes instead of by explicit pronouncements. The doctrine of artistic impersonality lying behind this technique and most commonly associated with Joyce and Eliot finds its discursive analogue in Frazer's calm, impartial, scholarly detachment. With it, he could survey man's entire history and find it a record of incalculable folly while contemplating the destruction of his own theories with complete equanimity.

Even more striking is the extent of modern literature's attraction to cyclical theories of life, history, and culture. *A Vision* and *Finnegans Wake* both celebrate this concept with elaborate care and a wealth of detail even as does *The Golden Bough* which not only links the astronomical, vegetative, and human worlds in a pattern of birth, flowering, death, and revival, but also closes where it began, namely, with the sacred grove at Nemi. In Frazer's tracing of this pattern an integral part was played by repetition of facts and restatement of hypotheses and inferences. The effect was not simply one of calling to mind points in danger of being lost sight of, but also of bearing in on the reader a sense of their profound significance, of their right to a brooding and thoughtful contemplation. And though it is undoubtedly the product of a particular and individual attitude toward the actual process of writing fiction, yet just the same sort of effect is achieved by Lawrence in the almost ritualistically repetitive passages of his novels such as *The Rainbow* and *The Plumed Serpent*. Lawrence, like Joyce and Eliot, also finds man's life represented symbolically in commonplace and traditional acts. For them as well as for Frazer, harvesting, love-making, bearing the sins of others, and performing the menial deeds of daily life, all reflect in different ways what is taken to be the essence of life. And to convey this complex essence, works like *The Waste Land, Ulysses, Finnegans Wake,* and *The Anathemata* rely heavily, even as does *The Golden Bough,* on a multiple series of cross-references and allusions which continually underscore the contemporaneity of all time.

From these stylistic and structural affinities between *The Golden Bough* and modern literature it is clear that even if Frazer's work was not directly imitated, was not a consciously employed source, it would still have exercised an influence on creative artists because of the imagination and technique exhibited. With this point, the last aspect of what I have called the literary reason for *The Golden Bough's* success comes into view. For though a sketch has been made of how and why Frazer rather than Farnell or Cook or Miss Harrison or Crawley or Hartland spearheaded the drive of comparative religion into literature, this still leaves the question of why *The Golden Bough* is preeminent among his works. The answer lies in its genre or literary mode, for in essence it is less a compendium of facts than a gigantic quest romance couched in the form of objective research. It is this basically archetypal consideration that reveals *The Golden*

Bough's impact on literature to be not fortuitous but necessary and inevitable. One has but to compare its opening pages with those of *Folklore in the Old Testament, The Fear of the Dead in Primitive Religion,* or *Myths of the Origin of Fire*[11] to see that in the former there is much more than simply discursive writing. The latter plunge immediately and prosaically into their subject:

> Attentive readers of the Bible can hardly fail to remark a striking discrepancy between the two accounts of the creation of man recorded in the first and second chapters of Genesis. [*FOT*]

> Men commonly believe that their conscious being will not end at death, but that it will be continued for an indefinite time or for ever, long after the frail corporeal envelope which lodged it for a time has mouldered in the dust. [*FOD*]

> Of all human inventions the discovery of the method of kindling fire has probably been the most momentous and far-reaching. It must date from an extreme antiquity, since there appears to be no well-attested case of a savage tribe ignorant of the use of fire and of the mode of producing it. [*MOF*]

With *The Golden Bough,* however, rhetorical question, alliteration, allusion, metaphor, inversion, all are enlisted to create a genuine literary experience, what the Joyce of *Finnegans Wake* might have called an "anthropoetic" experience:

> Who does not know Turner's picture of the Golden Bough? The scene, suffused with the golden glow of imagination in which the divine mind of Turner steeped and transfigured even the fairest natural landscape, is a dreamlike vision of the little woodland lake of Nemi—"Diana's Mirror," as it was called by the ancients. No one who has

[11] *Folklore in the Old Testament* (New York: Macmillan, 1918), I, 3; *The Fear of the Dead* (New York: Macmillan, 1933), I, 3; *Myths of the Origins of Fire* (New York: Macmillan, 1930), p. 1.

seen that calm water, lapped in a green hollow of the Alban hills, can ever forget it. The two characteristic Italian villages which slumber on its banks, and the equally Italian palace whose terraced gardens descend steeply to the lake, hardly break the stillness and even the solitariness of the scene. Dian herself might still linger by this lonely shore, still haunt these woodlands wild.

In antiquity this sylvan landscape was the scene of a strange and recurring tragedy. In order to understand it aright we must try to form in our minds an accurate picture of the place where it happened; for, as we shall see later on, a subtle link subsisted between the natural beauty of the spot and the dark crimes which under the mask of religion were often perpetrated there, crimes which after the lapse of so many ages still lend a touch of melancholy to these quiet woods and waters, like a chill breath of autumn on one of those bright September days "while not a leaf seems faded." [I, 1–2]

Granted that *The Golden Bough* is more carefully, more imaginatively written than his other works (passages in *The Worship of Nature* and his edition of *Pausanius* may be exceptions), this does not in itself make the book a romance rather than the encyclopaedic argument we have always thought it to be. One obvious connection between it and the traditional romance that most readers feel in some measure is suggested by the applicability to both of Ezra Pound's comment: "There are few people who can read more than a dozen or so of medieval romances, by Crestien or anyone else, without being over-wearied by the continual recurrence of the same or similar incidents, told in a similar manner."[12] Equally apparent and probably more significant is their joint development of themes out of a substratum of Nature myth and fertility ideals, their use of confla-

---

[12] Ezra Pound, *The Spirit of Romance* (Norfolk, Conn.: New Directions, 1952), p. 82.

tion and linking by means of central leit-motifs, their merging of incongruous materials, and their readiness to hint at possible meanings without spelling them out in detail.

And if we bear in mind that *The Golden Bough* is an instance of what Northrop Frye calls displacement, we can see certain additional features that both stamp it as a romance and account for its impact.[13] First, it, like the medieval romances, clearly deals with a quest—in this case, a quest to discover the meaning of the ritual observed by the priest of Diana, the King of the Wood, at Nemi. This fact alone almost explains Frazer's seminal role in modern literature, for the thematic quests of Eliot for redemption, Joyce for a father, Lawrence for a Golden Age, Yeats for the buried treasure or hidden mystery, and Miss Sitwell for purification are all adumbrated in *The Golden Bough*. While Frazer announces his quest from the beginning and completes it just prior to rounding off the narrative, he does not follow the pure romance in regarding this as the major adventure led up to by a series of minor incidents and forming the climax of his story. Instead he pulls the traditional formula inside out by beginning and ending with a secondary encounter while gradually working in toward the central experiences he is dealing with, which are those of crucifixion and resurrection. The effects which result are highly instructive for modern literature.

For one thing Frazer's de-emphasizing of plot and narrative continuity parallels much modern fiction. Nowhere is this parallel more thoroughgoing than in the tendency of both to locate their climaxes, their central, crucial experiences, in incidents of discovery or revelation almost totally devoid of action. Thus, the notion of what might be called the important unimportant situation or event, which has become a stock device of the contem-

---

[13] *Anatomy of Criticism* (Princeton: Princeton University Press, 1957), pp. 136–137, 365.

porary short story, is one of the organizing principles of *The Golden Bough*.

The same reversal of the romance pattern also provides another effect central to modern literature. Thematically, it consists of the gradual accrual of meaning as the reader follows a trail of hints and artistically incomplete bits of information. Just as Frazer extends *anagnorisis* virtually throughout the entire book so do *The Sound and the Fury, Absalom, Absalom!,* the major novels of Henry James, and the "Alexandria Quartet." Structurally, the reversal provides the idea of pattern by piecemeal. This is based on a dislocation of perspective which brings us too close to the scene or overwhelms us with detail so that only when we stand back and regard the whole work does the pattern emerge. Instances of this which come readily to mind are *Finnegans Wake, The Cantos,* and Dos Passos' *U. S. A.* Frazer achieves precisely the same thing, both thematically and structurally, when we are forced to follow him through a tangle of magicians' arts, species of taboo, and perils of the soul before coming upon one of his central topics—the death and resurrection of gods—in Volumes IV and V. By focusing on these volumes rather than others, *The Waste Land* showed how much more profound its grasp was of *The Golden Bough* than was that of Ronald Bottrall's *Festivals of Fire.* But not even the *Adonis, Attis, Osiris* segments provide the whole core, for only in Volume VIII on *The Scapegoat* do we catch a glimpse of the earlier books' complementary theme, that of the crucifixion of gods and men.

We are told that the romance proper projects the ideals of the ruling social or intellectual class; that its quest has three stages (conflict, death, and discovery or resolution); that this threefold structure is repeated in many other features; that the quest involves two central characters (a protagonist and an antagonist); that the secondary characters are simplified and weak in outline; that the quest's most frequent goals are the slaying of a dragon and the acquisition of wealth in some form; and that the romance possesses a number of distinguishable types of phases.[14] Now not only does *The Golden Bough* have a quest motif as a dominant feature, but it also exhibits all of the characteristics just mentioned, though obviously not in the same way as they appear in *Perceval,* the *Perlesvaus,* or *Sir Gawain and the Green Knight.*

Unlike the medieval romances, *The Golden Bough* does not embody the ideals of an aristocratic, feudal society, but it does convey a clear sense of the values that dominated the post-Darwinian, rationalistic ethos of late nineteenth-century England. Reason and truth are to Frazer what mystic love was to von Strassburg, chivalric honor to Chretien, or Christian faith to von Eschenbach. Thus, in what stands as a proem to his tale of adventure he suggests the comparative approach has not only intrinsic intellectual significance but social usefulness derived from an unswerving adherence to truth. As a result, the real hero or protagonist of *The Golden Bough* proves to be the civilized mind which explores uncharted ways to uncover new and unknown facts about man's way of life, facts which may be simultaneously horrifying, engrossing, and revolutionary. In short, the hero is Frazer himself, who, like Nero Wolf, solved the mysterious puzzles and crimes of mankind from an armchair. If this sedentary role seems to violate the notion of the quest or marvelous journey as central to the romance, we may recall that the wanderer was as frequently a book as an author. The varied and widely dispersed forms of folk tales, ballads, and romances are cases in point.[15] However pertinent to anthropology Andrew Lang's jibe was about Covent Garden experts, it is clearly irrelevant to *The Golden Bough* as a romance.

To find the answer to the sacred kingship of Italy in Southern India, as Frazer claims to have done, is in the best tradition of

---

[14] *Anatomy of Criticism,* pp. 186–202.
[15] *Anatomy of Criticism,* p. 57.

the Grail knights who travel into distant lands seeking the goal
of their quest. Like them, Frazer found himself almost insensibly
embarked upon his wanderings. As he says, "wider and wider
prospects opened out before me; and thus step by step I was
lured into far-spreading fields" (I, vii). The same basic image of
the journey that is a quest provides the controlling frame of the
entire book. In the first chapter the rational hero decides that
"the survey of a wider field" may "contain in germ the solution
of the problem" (I, 42–43). And like Jason, Theseus, or Odysseus,
he offers his listening companions "a voyage of discovery, in
which we shall visit many strange foreign lands, with strange
foreign peoples, and still stranger customs. The wind is in the
shrouds: we shake out our sails to it, and leave the coast of
Italy behind us for a time" (I, 43). Eleven volumes and over a
hundred chapters later, with all of these predictions fulfilled,
Frazer announces the end of the quest: "Our long voyage of
discovery is over and our bark has drooped her weary sails in
port at last" (XI, 308).

Within this frame of journey and incredible adventure both
the quest and the central characters of *The Golden Bough* reveal
their affinities with romance. Frazer's quest possesses the requisite
three stages, though naturally blurred by his assumption he was
writing anthropology rather than literature. Secondary variations
on this triple form are the book's three major subjects (magic
and the sacred kingship, the principles of taboo, and the myth
and ritual of the Dying God) and its three editions, the latter
being equivalent, I imagine, to the romance hero's success on his
third attempt. As for the quest stages themselves, they traditionally involve an extended conflict between the protagonist and
his antagonist, a vital confrontation in which at least one is
slain, and finally the discovery and exaltation of the hero which
provides a dramatic resolution to the quest. In *The Golden
Bough* the conflict is waged over human beliefs and customs.
More particularly, two antagonistic forces try to settle whether or

not there is any connection between various species of religious beliefs or between religious customs generally and those usually thought of as wholly secular. Frazer as the protagonist advances the cause of unaided reason and objective scientific truth against the entrenched powers of superstition whose key representative is the man of religious faith. In one sense, like the Grail legend itself, *The Golden Bough* is the fruit of a crusade, though as Robert Graves keeps reiterating, a highly discreet and covert crusade.[16] The similarity to the romance pattern is heightened by Frazer's suggesting his task is to help his society rid itself of afflictions and weaknesses emanating from a powerful and aged adversary who lives "in a strong tower" and who will not hesitate to tempt the hero with appeals to antiquity, expediency, and beauty (I, xxv–xxvi).

Though the conflict of reason and faith or science and religion is perhaps endless, *The Golden Bough* imaginatively envisages the second quest stage, that of the death of one of the combatants. In this case, the defeat is dealt to the representative of tradition and faith whom Frazer calls superstition. And while it is difficult to say just precisely at what point in the book this occurs, one would probably not be far wrong in locating the instant of fatality in the note on "The Crucifixion of Christ" appended to the ninth volume. Showing that Christ died as the annual representative of a god whose counterparts were well known all over Western Asia, Frazer intimates, "will reduce Jesus of Nazareth to the level of a multitude of other victims of a barbarous superstition, and will see in him no more than a moral teacher, whom the fortunate accident of his execution invested with the crown, not merely of a martyr, but of a god" (IX, 422–423). Here Frazer joins forces with Nietzsche, for in his

[16] Helen Adolf, *Visio Pacis* (University Park: Pennsylvania State University Press, 1960), p. 11; Robert Graves, *Occupation: Writer* (New York: Creative Age Press, 1950), pp. 42–43.

account of the death of a god he is slaying his antagonist who is god. As for the third stage, that of discovery, exaltation, and resolution, it occurs most unmistakably in the penultimate chapter of the entire study. Here Frazer finally discovers the link between the golden bough and the mistletoe which enables him to resolve his quest by finding a generic explanation for the exploits of Aeneas, Balder, and the Kings of the Wood at Nemi. And in so doing, he has, in effect, achieved his exaltation as a hero who completes his task and also guaranteed his recognition by his own as well as a later generation.

Traditionally the three-stage quest of the romance is directed to the slaying of a dragon and the finding of buried treasure. When we turn to *The Golden Bough,* we encounter enough dragons and treasure for scores of romances, but these don't seem to be exactly what we are after, if only because they exist in no direct, active relation to our hero, Sir James. A useful clue here is Northrop Frye's suggestion that the labyrinth is an image of the dragon or monster.[17] To anyone who has observed *The Golden Bough's* technique of circling around and around its particular subjects—as, say, when the identification of the mistletoe as the elusive golden bough is reached after consideration of taboos concerning the earth and sun, the seclusion of girls at puberty, fire-festivals, magic flowers, the varied locations and nature of external souls, and the myth of Balder—it is clear that here is a labyrinth of gigantic size and complexity. Pretty clearly the myth underlying *The Golden Bough*—the myth beneath the myths as it were—is that of Theseus and the Minotaur. The monster, then, which Frazer the rational hero seeks to slay is ignorance itself whose archetypal form is a half-human, half-animal composite of ancient myth, modern folklore, and the ritual customs of both past and present. Thus, the monster is intellectual: the puzzle created by the impingement of irrational or inade-

[17] *Anatomy of Criticism,* p. 190.

192

quate explanations on the rational mind rooted in common-sense.

Frazer's characteristic reaction to the monster is seen at the very outset when he remarks that "it needs no elaborate demonstration to convince us that the stories told to account for Diana's worship at Nemi are unhistorical" (I, 21). Coupled with this is his determination to conquer his adversary by framing rational questions to be answered with the aid of his famed weapon, the comparative method. The result is his entry into the labyrinth in pursuit of the protean monster, an event dramatized by such remarks as "we must try to *probe deeper* by examining the worship as well as the legend or myth of Hippolytus" (I, 24) (italics mine). To guarantee his return he pays out behind him a slender chain of hypotheses, conjectures, and common-sense assumptions. His reward is not only the destroying (at least to his own satisfaction) of falsehood and superstition but the acquisition of the treasure buried deep in the labyrinth. For the scholar such as Frazer the ideal form of wealth is knowledge ordered into a coherent form and issuing in the wisdom of revelation, in this case, of "the long march, the slow and toilsome ascent, of humanity from savagery to civilisation" (I, xxv).

While much more could be said about *The Golden Bough* as a displaced quest romance—for instance, its complex use of pity and fear as forms of pleasure so that the appropriate romance strains of the marvellous, a thoughtful melancholy, and a tender, passive charm are pervasive[18]—enough has been said to suggest the plausibility of the identification. There still remains one final point to be faced. Even if *The Golden Bough* is a quest romance, how does this account for its importance to modern literature? Obviously important aspects in any answer would be its quest motif, religious significance, and archetypal symbolism. But modern literature has also been marked by a profoundly ironic temper which would seem at odds with the ideal-

---

[18] *Anatomy of Criticism*, p. 37.

ized world of romance. This point brings us back to features of the problem already mentioned—the style and structure of *The Golden Bough*. Though doubtless the pure romance has little affinity with irony, it is also true that the romances closest to us in time, whether of Hawthorne or Hudson, usually possess a considerable admixture of irony. And the same is true of *The Golden Bough*. It was not for nothing that Frazer found his prose masters in Anatole France and Ernest Renan.

One of our most sensitive critics has pointed out Joyce's use of Renan's combination of irony and pity, and the same is true too of *The Golden Bough*.[19] It opens with "a dream-like vision" (I, 1) of Nemi in which descriptive charm expresses a tender pity for the human follies enacted there. From this it immediately modulates into a compound irony based on the relation of man and god, which if not central is at least typical: "In the civil war its [Nemi's] sacred treasures went to replenish the empty coffers of Octavian, who well understood the useful art of thus securing the divine assistance, if not the divine blessing, for the furtherance of his ends. But we are not told that he treated Diana on this occasion as civilly as his divine uncle Julius Caesar once treated Capitoline Jupiter himself, borrowing three thousand pounds' weight of solid gold from the god, and scrupulously paying him back with the same weight of gilt copper" (I, 4).

More germane to Frazer's central aim is his use of the comparative method for ironic purposes. Irony by incongruous juxtaposition undeniably reentered English literature with a heavy French accent, but one should not overlook the way in which Frazer's celebrated method frequently performed the same function on a broader level. Nor is it without significance that T. S. Eliot and Edith Sitwell, the two most assiduous students of Laforgue and Corbière, were also attentive readers of *The Golden*

---

[19] Harry Levin, *James Joyce* (Norfolk, Conn.: New Directions, 1941), p. 217.

Bough. One version of Frazer's technique is the large-scale juxtaposition of ostensibly opposed but similar rites, as with the festivals of Adonis and St. John (IV, 244ff). Another is that of the sober understatement of a hypothesis such as when he observes that "there is no intrinsic improbability in the view that for the sake of edification the church may have converted a real heathen festival into a nominal Christian one" (I, 16). Even more oblique yet pervasive is his use of terms and images that ironically expose similarities his opponent seeks to conceal, as when a worshipper of Artemis is said to pay tithes to the goddess or when it is noted that Cybele and Attis were worshipped on the site of the Vatican. And finally there is irony employed for comic purposes and directed at his own controlling concepts, like that of the dying and reviving god. Thus, in a passage such as the following we may discern the lineaments of Joyce's ironic handling of Christian rites in *Ulysses* and his more jocular chronicling of H. C. E.'s rise and fall: "in his long and chequered career this mythical personage has displayed a remarkable tenacity of life. For we can hardly doubt that the Saint Hippolytus of the Roman calendar, who was dragged by horses to death on the thirteenth of August, Diana's own day, is no other than the Greek hero of the same name, who after dying twice over as a heathen sinner has been happily resuscitated as a Christian saint" (I, 21).

Like that of modern literature as a whole, Frazer's irony begins in realism with a wry recognition of human folly and broadens out into a mythic treatment of men who imitate gods, are sacrificed to the needs of society, seize and hold power through unscrupulous stratagems and a shrewd knowledge of mass psychology, and abase themselves in obedience to one whom they fancy greater than themselves. Thus, if we take Hardy, Huxley, Lawrence, and Joyce as typifying recent modes of irony, we can see how *The Golden Bough* encompasses their moods of fatalism, anger, nostalgia, and detachment and integrates them into an encyclopaedic vision of the knowledge inherent in its society. In effect, then, *The Golden Bough* became central to twentieth century literature because it was grounded in the essential realism of anthropological research, informed with the romance quest of an ideal, and controlled by the irony in divine myth and human custom. Together these made it the discursive archetype and hence matrix of that literature.

The papers comprising *Myth and Symbol* were selected by a committee consisting of Professor Bernice Slote, chairman, University of Nebraska; Professor Alfredo Roggiano, State University of Iowa; and the Editor of the University of Nebraska Press.

Officers of the Midwest Modern Language Association

President:

1961–1962	1962–1963
James E. Miller, Jr.	John S. Brushwood
University of Nebraska	University of Missouri

Vice-President:

Frank D. Hirschbach	Donald Emerson
University of Minnesota	University of Wisconsin, Milwaukee

Secretary-Treasurer:

Ferman Bishop	Ferman Bishop
Illinois State Normal University	Illinois State Normal University

Officers of the Central Renaissance Conference

President:

Robert E. Knoll	Charles F. Mullett
University of Nebraska	University of Missouri

Secretary:

Philipp Fehl	Charles Nauert
University of Nebraska	University of Missouri